Getting Things Done

SECOND EDITION

When

You Are Not In Charge

GEOFFREY M. BELLMAN

BK

BERRETT-KOEHLER PUBLISHERS, INC.
San Francisco

Berrett-Koehler Publishers, Inc.
235 Montgomery Street, Suite 650
San Francisco, CA 94104-2916
Tel: 415-288-0260   Fax: 415-362-2512
Website: www.bkconnection.com

ORDERING INFORMATION

Individual sales. Berrett-Koehler publications are available through most bookstores. They can also be ordered direct from Berrett-Koehler Publishers by calling, toll-free: 800-929-2929; fax 802-864-7626.

Quantity sales. Special discounts are available on quantity purchases by corporations, associations, and others. For details, contact the "Special Sales Department" at the Berrett-Koehler address above.

Orders for college textbook/course adoption use. Please contact Berrett-Koehler Publishers toll-free: 800-929-2929; fax 802-864-7626.

Orders by U.S. trade bookstores and wholesalers. Please contact Publishers Group West, 1700 Fourth Street, Berkeley, CA 94710; 510-528-1444; 1-800-788-3123; fax 510-528-9555.

Printed in the United States of America

Library of Congress Cataloging-in-Publication Data
Bellman, Geoffrey M., 1938–
   Getting things done when you are not in charge / by Geoffrey M. Bellman.—2nd ed.
      p. cm.
   Includes bibliographical references and index.
   ISBN 1-57675-172-4
   1. Leadership. 2. Executive ability. 3. Organizational effectiveness. I. Title.
   HD57.7.B454 2001
   658.4′292—dc21   2001025441

06 05 04 03 02 01   10 9 8 7 6 5 4 3 2

Developmental editor: Sheila Kelly
Copyeditor: Judith Johnstone
Text design: Detta Penna
Compositor/production service: Penna Design & Production
Indexer: Joan Dickey

To
Michaela,
Joshua,
and
Geoffrey

Contents

Preface   *xi*
What This New Edition Is About / Why I Wrote This Book /
Who Is This Book For / How To Read This Book /
Acknowledgments

Introduction: You Are Not In Charge   *1*
The Illusion: Someone Is In Charge / The Life Game

Chapter 1: A Model For Getting Things Done   *5*
An Exercise: Drawing Your Life 8 / What To Read Next

Chapter 2: "Why Is That Important?"   *11*
An Exercise: What Is Important 14

Chapter 3: Pursuing Your Aspirations   *17*
Know What You Want / Know *Why* You Want What You
Want / Wants Are Linked to Life Purpose / Figure Out What
You Want Before Talking About It / Each Day Remind Yourself
of What Is Important / Alignment of Wants Builds Power /
Lead Your Own Life / Immediate Fulfillment Requires
Immediate Action / Distant Fulfillment Requires Persistence /
Know *How* You Want To Work With Others

Chapter 4: Discovering Dreams   *25*
Wants Always Exist / Express The Dream / Discover What
They Want That You Want / Build Commitment To Wants /
Reinvent The Wheel / Help Them Know That You Know /
Collaboration and Negotiation: Your Best Options /
Competition and Avoidance: Not Your Best Options

Chapter 5: What Is Really Happening?   *33*
Five Steps To Discovering Reality / **An Exercise: Organizational Reality 37** / Love of the Bumps

Chapter 6: Build Common Understanding   *41*
Help Others Find and Face the Truth / The Organizational Village / Building Understanding In Organizations

Chapter 7: Face The Politics   *47*
Politics Are Real and Inescapable / My Kind of Politics / Your Mix of Politics and Values / Building a Positive Political Climate / Working Through Negative Political Situations

Chapter 8: Seek The Priorities   *55*
Follow the Money / Trace the Time / Find Your Power / **An Exercise: Building Formal Power 59**

Chapter 9: Who Makes A Difference?   *61*
An Exercise: Successful Work Relationships 63 / Help Those Whom You Would Have Help You / Respect the Past / Deal Openly / Create Your Relationship Web

Chapter 10: Enlist Able Partners   *69*
The Parts In Partnership / Anticipating Success / Contracts and Contracting / Your Unique Value-Added Contribution / Partnership Begins With You / Build a Pattern of Accomplishments / Pass the Word on Your Success / Expect Less Appreciation / Accept Others' Lack of Knowledge / Ask About What They Care About / Risk Seeing It Their Way / Say Yes . . . And Say No / Long-Term Partnerships / Summary

Chapter 11: Controlling Work Dynamics   *83*
A Model For Working With You / Our Need To Control

Chapter 12: Dealing With Decision Makers   *89*
Show and Earn Respect / **An Exercise: Building Respect 90** / They Don't Understand Your Work / Understand Their Purpose and Viewpoint / Do Not Wait: Initiate! / Link Your Work To Key Systems / Seek Reviews of Your Work / Find Ways To Offer Feedback / Summary

Chapter 13: How Might You Help?   *99*

An Exercise: Self Discovery 101 / I vs. They / Out There vs. In Here / Learning The Truth About Yourself / Knowledge of Your Self

Chapter 14: Find The Courage To Risk   *107*

The Risks of Stepping Forward / Putting Fears In Perspective / **Three Exercises: Building Your Courage 114–117** / Summary

Chapter 15: Making Your Work Rewarding   *119*

Reaction and Reward / The Rewards of Membership / Making Your Work Rewarding / Praise Fixation Breeds Dependence / **An Exercise: Rewards From Your Work 124**

Chapter 16: Create Change   *127*

Stability Meets Instability / The Need For Change Must Be Compelling / Leading Change Is Demanding / Change Is Rooted In Respect / Help Others Hear Your Ideas / Resistance Reveals Power / Perseverance Required / Ideas Must Find Their Time / The Dangers of Rapid Change / Change In Changing Organizations / Succeed On Their Terms As Well As Your Own / Expect The Change To Allow You To Be Yourself

Chapter 17: Actions That Get Things Done   *139*

Twenty Actions To Get Things Done / Building on and Beyond This Book

Conclusion: A Life Perspective On Leading Change   *145*

Resources   *147*

Index   *149*

About the Author   *155*

Preface

You are not in charge. You may not be clear who *is* in charge, but you know that you are not. In spite of this, you want to do your work well, you want to contribute to the organization, and you want to succeed personally. These wants often cause conflict, as you are challenged to support others' goals while working toward your own. You feel irritated by the difficulty of trying to get something done and not having the power to do it. You feel constrained by the formal and informal boundaries of the organization. You try to do your best, but keep running up against the rules of play in the organization you are trying to help. You may work in the profit or not-for-profit sector. You may give your time or work for money. You may be a manager, a director, a salaried or an hourly worker. It does not matter. You share with many others the desire to do good work, the need for recognition, and the frustration of having your efforts blocked by the very organization you are trying to serve.

You are not as powerless as you sometimes feel: that is the main premise of this book. This book explores the many ways you can get things done, support the work of others, and find greater life fulfillment through your work. There are ways of dealing with the issues inherent in working for an organization. I know the issues well after thirty-five years in and around organizations. I have lived with the dilemmas of working from the middle of large corporations, government agencies, school systems, hospitals, foundations, and not-for-profit organizations. I have had amazing success and sobering failure, and I have learned. This book builds on my learning, and on the learning of others with whom I have worked, and it can be a guide to your learning as well. It is my answer to the question "How can you feel good about your work and make a difference when you have little formal power?"

Organizations loom large in our lives; you know the struggles that come with working in them. You know what it is like to have clear, constructive intentions and to be confounded by the way this place works. You know how hard it is to hold onto hope while faced with daily frustrations. You know the stress, the burnout, the fatigue, and you have felt yourself alternately rising to the challenge or sinking into skepticism. You see those frequent "learning opportunities" that come with trying to get something done, and sometimes feel that you have learned enough—it is somebody else's turn. You know the energy it takes to step back into the fray, and are tempted just to save your energy and protect yourself. This book helps your pursuit of the hope, the challenge, the opportunity, and the learning from right where you are now, in your formally less-powerful position.

"I am not in charge." Can you hear yourself saying these words? Say them aloud or in your mind: What do you sound like? What was your tone of voice? How did you feel? When did you last say something like this to someone about your work? As I have listened to myself and others say these words, I sort the statements and their underlying feelings into two stacks: One stack sounds more active, hopeful, or even matter-of-fact; the other sounds more passive, powerless, or even victimized. Over my many work years, I have contributed to both stacks . . . and guess which stack I feel better about.

If you are not in charge, who is? That is a good question. You will see, as you read further, that I doubt any one person is truly in charge. We create a sense of purpose and responsibility together, and we do it in ways that make us all interdependent—whether we choose to see it that way or not. Everyone is accountable to others, and that accountability circles back within the boundaries of an organization, helping to define what it is and what it does. We point to the CEO's or ED's or Chairs as if they are in charge, but that is more our wish for simplicity and security than it is an expression of reality. We maintain the "in-chargeness" that selected people experience for organizational convenience; we know just how much and how little they are really in charge of. We agree to putting some people "in charge," knowing that they have to earn the support of the people around them if they are to get anything done.

If anyone is in charge around here, it is the top executive, right? Well, no. In my close work with the leaders of many organizations, I have noticed the direct relationship between their effectiveness and not being in charge. Said differently, those executives who constantly behave as if they are in charge are not nearly as effective as those who act as if they are not.

What This New Edition Is About

Fifteen years ago, I wrote what I thought was my first and last book on getting things done from the middle of large organizations. That book was titled *The Quest for Staff Leadership*; it was written for the managers of service and support functions in corporate America. The book was well received, went through five printings, and even received a national award. Six years later I revised the book significantly, wrote it to a wider audience—everyone in support positions in the corporate world. And here I am rewriting it yet again, and reaching out beyond the corporate world to everyone in the middle of organizations of any kind. This rewriting, moving from book two to book three, is just as significant as the move from book one to book two. There are two main reasons: what has been happening in the organization world and what I have learned along the way.

In the fifteen years since book one, the organization world has been chaotic. Reading over my earlier versions reminded me of how much the organizational world has changed in less than a generation. Information technology and systems, cyberspace, mergers, acquisitions and divestitures, virtual teams, global marketplace, generation X, politics, prosperity, recession, dot.coms, shifting demography, aging population, health care, education, and you could add to the list. Change is in the air. It is disrupting everything and everyone who tries to remain static, and it looks as if this unpredictable untidiness will continue indefinitely. All of this external change profoundly affects the ways we get things done, and makes working successfully from the middle even more important than ever before.

I have added fifteen years to my work experience, and I have added years of not-for-profit experience to my years with for-profits. I've had more time to watch for patterns. I've learned more about what allows people to thrive in the middle of organizations, and I am more encouraged than ever about the opportunities present in today's emerging organizations for the able, invested individual. This new book might better be called an adaptation than a new edition. Not a paragraph has gone untouched; much of it is brand new. The entire book has been refocused, rewritten, and reordered.

Why I Wrote This Book

Work is central, whether you are telecommuting from home, or traveling with an electronic tether back to the office, or showing up daily to pursue the same work in the same cubicle, or giving hours a week to your community. Work is a primary way to develop yourself while contributing to the world. You have the opportunity to pursue your life's meaning through working, and this book was written to help you in that pursuit. There ought to be more to life in an organization than just "earning a living" or "doing your duty." Work offers the real possibility of accomplishing something wonderful for yourself, for the people you work with, for the organization you serve, and even for the community and world beyond. Through this book I will help you to consider what you want to accomplish and to do something about it.

Your effectiveness in your various tasks and your power with the others with whom you work, comes from your sense of work's importance in your life. Your enthusiasm for your work and your delight with your contribution are directly connected to your sense that this work has meaning in your life. This book is infused with the essential importance of work to our lives; we have the opportunity (free or forced) to work and discover ourselves in the process. Our daily practical choices can lead us toward the lives we want. The higher authority of our own life purpose can inform each decision we make in a way that gives us more success and happiness. At least, that is what I am reaching for through writing this book; I hope to be a guide for you in your work life. The practical choices and actions involved in doing this will become clear in later chapters.

Who Is This Book For?

If you regularly work with an organization—for money or for free—and you want to succeed for the sake of the organization and of yourself, then this book is for you. All you need to bring is the willingness to improve yourself and the organization. You do not need a high salary or position; you do not need a diploma or a desk. But you do need to bring yourself and the belief that your work can be a source of happiness. Many of our most successful workers *love* working. It's not unusual to find two people working side by side, where she loves her work and he hates it—and both have the same job. What makes the difference? It is clearly not the nature of the work itself; it has more to do with how people approach it. And how they approach others. These two people with exactly the same roles have made regular choices about how they will deal with others, and each choice has its own consequences. These two people choose how they see their roles, and that choice too has consequences. All of this is played out within an organization culture full of expectations and assumptions about the people working there, yielding even more consequences. This book is for people who relish—or would like to relish—going to work each day because their work holds promise. Rather than wasting their breath complaining about their lack of formal power, they build their personal power and get things done.

How to Read This Book

I have written this book for the busy person who seldom reads a book from cover to cover. After the introduction and first chapter, go where your current issues and interests take you. I did not write the book in the order you find it, and you do not have to read it sequentially. Open it to a random chapter and start reading. You will find that most chapters, after first guiding your thinking to a few key points, offer examples, actions, and exercises that help you think more deeply about your work—and maybe even do something about it.

Acknowledgments

Life does not allow us to succeed on our own; others are essential in defining who we are. I am especially indebted to the many organizations with whom I have worked as an employee or a consultant, for pay or for free, over the last thirty-five years. They taught me how to work with them. Whatever you find useful here, I learned there. I appreciate the experienced eyes and professional minds who critiqued the first edition of this book and suggested what I might do this time: Thank you Allan Paulson, Kathleen Webb Tunney, Frank Basler, Cathie Leavitt, and Jeff Pym. Sheila Kelly did the editing; she is a joy to work with—and even more fun to be married to. Steve Piersanti and his company, Berrett-Koehler Publishers, treat me in ways that most authors only dream of. It is a privilege to work with him again, on this our fifth book together.

Geoff Bellman
Seattle
March 2001

You Are Not In Charge

We succeed by helping others succeed; our accomplishment is dependent on theirs. In our more expansive moments, we might say that we make them successful. In their more generous moments, they might say that they couldn't do it without us. We are often in-between, wondering how best to contribute and how much difference we make. Some of us get trapped "on hold," waiting for the authority, waiting for others to tell us what to do. That does not work.

Our only chance for contributing is to quit waiting and wondering and *do something*. We serve ourselves and others best when we do not wait. Initiate, with the organization and all involved people in mind. No, we are not in charge but we can act. No, we are not formally designated leaders, but we can lead. This book will help you think of yourself as a leader, as someone who helps an organization, its people, and resources move in new directions. Yes, right from where you are, not waiting until you've moved into a more powerful position. Whether you are an individual contributor, a middle manager, a school principal, or a precinct chair, there is much you can do from your position right there in the middle of things. Whether you are an entering programmer, a journeyman mechanic, a PTA parent, or a social worker, you can choose to lead others. And, the first step in leading others at work is leading your own life.

The Illusion: Someone Is in Charge

Many of us grew up with the expectation that someone will watch over us, take care of us, be "in charge," "know best," and that this will turn out okay. Our families, schools, communities, and organizations taught us to believe this, but their teachings began to fray pretty early, usually before we became adults. Our contradictory experience confused us; we saw people "in charge" producing very mixed results. The people in position to "do what's best" disappointed us. Programs they created, decisions they made, did not turn out okay—at least not for us and what we wanted out of our lives. We discovered that they would *not* watch over us. An extremely hard part of this learning is not our disappointment in them but our struggles with our own responsibility: If they are not in charge, who is? If I cannot count on them, who can I count on? What is my responsibility in helping my family, my community, my employer, or this world? What can I, what *will* I, do with my life? These are the big questions lurking behind the work questions we struggle with daily.

You may be thinking, "But someday I *will* be in charge of that committee (or agency or division or team) and I *will* change things!" Well, think again. That's akin to getting married with the plan to start changing your spouse immediately after the ceremony. My research says that does not work very well. I have often heard executives lament about their difficulties in getting things done. When the president of a telecommunications company (with 23,000 employees across five states and nine hierarchical levels) first saw this book, he said "Finally, a book written for me!" His employees may not see him as not in charge, but he frequently feels that way. He knows the limitations of authority. It is too easy for us to attribute power to a position that we have yet to hold, or that others hold, and to diminish the power we currently have. This book works with the powers we now hold.

The Life Game

For a few minutes, imagine your life as a game with rules and goals, roles and scores. Life is much more complicated than a game, but temporarily imagine playing Life as you might play bridge, or *Myst*™, or soccer. Within this game called Life, you decide its purposes and rules. You decide the roles you will play; you decide what earns points; you keep score. Actions that move you toward your life goals earn points. Actions that move you away from your life goals lose points. You create the game of Life as you play it; you can change the rules. Unpredictable, uncontrollable, unreasonable outside forces influence Life. You are in the middle of Life now; you are playing.

That is how life works when seen through the simpler game metaphor. It is the largest of the many games we play: games like School, Parent, Politics, Citizen, Child, and Work. In this book, most of our attention will be directed at the game of Work as a subset of the game of Life—and the challenge of playing the two games while keeping Work subordinate to Life. Often, other people decide the explicit rules and goals for Work before you arrive. And you have implicitly decided the rules and goals of Life before you arrive to "play" Work. The challenge is engaging deeply with both games, and keeping Work within the larger context of Life. Five guides shape this book:

1. *Create your life game.* The secret of getting things done when you are not in charge is to establish a life larger than work, in which you are more in charge than at work. Without this larger, more important life game, you will end up playing by the rules of the work game, or reacting against them with no clear sense of purpose.

2. *Learn the work game.* There is a work game where you work. It has its own rules and roles, goals and penalties—whether you are aware of it or not. There are ways for people to succeed. Certain behaviors are respected; others are disparaged. Learn this. It is not a matter of liking but of understanding how this work game works.

3. *Know your position in the work game.* This allows you to know where you are starting from. Again, it does not mean that you like it, but that you understand what comes with the position you have. The best starting point for changing your position, or the work game, is to know what you are starting with. Of course, if you hate your position, you should not be playing here. Which leads to. . .

4. *Recognize there are other work games.* There are other places in this world of work where you could be offering your talents. All

of those other places have work games of their own. Choose the work game you play, always honoring your larger life game. If your life game is not being served by this work game, then go play somewhere else. Your ultimate power in the work game comes from *choosing* to play here, and knowing you make that choice daily.

5. *Play well and hard at both Work and Life.* Concentrate. Keep reminding yourself of what is important. Know your skills and your aspirations.

The most useful ideas in this book link back to this Life and Work game metaphor. Life direction is your source of power; options open when you see your work as a vital part of your life. Creating your life game is difficult; you are the game designer, rulemaker, player, coach, referee, scorekeeper, cheerleader, and spectator. Little wonder that we often opt to play others' games, winning and losing under rules they have made. Others can help us figure out Life, but no one else can play Life for us. A pattern of playing others' games usually calls us back to our own life game: What do we want to do with this life? And how might our work support that?

CHAPTER ONE

A Model for Getting Things Done

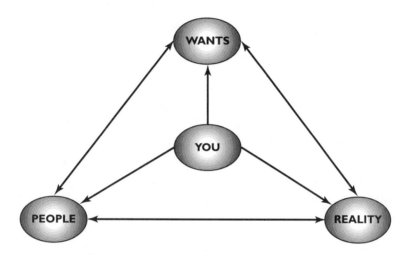

Often, what we need is a simple way to dig through the messiness of task forces, councils, or committees to which we belong. That's what this model is about. It gives us a way of sorting all the information that inundates us; it helps us decide what is important, and to sort it from what is not. Our hope of influencing our organizations increases when we have a way of understanding them. The Getting Things Done (GTD) model has been useful to many people over the years. You will see this GTD model repeatedly; it is the hook upon which the content of this book hangs. The model's usefulness is directly related to its simplicity. You can remember it in the middle of a meeting; you can use it to ask questions or to seek or sort the information you need. Or, you can use it to sort out issues within your own life. Or, an entire organization can pause to consider this model.

Consider the four elements of the GTD model:

- **WANTS:** This is the way you would like the world to be, the possible, the desirable, the potential world—and it is usually different from REALITY. The difference between WANTS and REALITY creates a tension.

- **REALITY:** This is how things are right now, the day-to-day world in which you and others live, with all its comforts and discomforts, joys and sorrows, satisfactions and dissatisfactions.

- **PEOPLE:** These are the individuals and groups that care about the world as it is (REALITY) and/or as it could be (WANT). They are a potential source of talent, energy, money, expertise, and other resources. They may be for or against what you want to do, and they are vital to it.

- **YOU:** You are in the middle of all of this with potential connections to the PEOPLE, WANTS, and REALITY. You are not in charge but you definitely want to get something done. Connecting the dots will create movement and help PEOPLE change REALITY to what they WANT.

This model puts *you* in the pivotal role. You are potentially powerful; you can connect the dots, making a solid change triangle. You are key to the change. But for this to happen, you have to step out of the PEOPLE corner and define yourself as someone who is willing to take action. Like the person in this example: A worker in a manufacturing plant noticed that disagreements between her shift and the next shift were increasing, reaching the point where they were blaming each other for everything and hardly talking. She decided to do something about it. She gathered a few key PEOPLE over coffee to begin to discuss the REALITY of what was going on and what they WANTED. They agreed that they all wanted work to be a more positive experience. They identified and agreed to work on two problems. None of this would have happened if that one worker had not separated herself from all of the PEOPLE and taken individual action. She brought the issue; she gathered the right people; they identified what they wanted and what they had; they took constructive action.

This example shows the GTD model in action, and it shows how the investment of one person can make a difference. That's what the model is about, making a positive difference in your work world, stepping out to help people move the present reality toward what you all want. This could be called a "change" model or a "leadership" model. Whether or not you think in terms of being a change agent or a leader, I do, and I will frequently talk in those terms in the coming chapters. The movement from REALITY toward WANTS is change, and YOU at the center of this model are a leader when you start hooking the three corners together.

Explore the four elements of the GTD model through these questions:

WANTS

Why is that important?

What do key people in this organization want?

What do their wants have in common?

How do their wants differ?

How committed are they to acting on their wants?

REALITY

What is really happening?

How do key people describe what exists right now?

What do their descriptions have in common?

How do their descriptions differ?

How responsible do they feel for the current state of affairs?

PEOPLE

Who makes a difference?

Who could be affected by the changes anticipated?

Who are the key people?

What are their special talents, resources, or powers?

How willing are they to work with each other?

YOU

How might you help?

What special talents, resources, or powers do you have?

Why do you want to change things?

How does your description of wants fit with others?

How does your description of reality fit with others?

How well do you work with the people involved?

The GTD model, along with the above questions, can help us to think before acting. There are more questions that could be asked; these are merely a sample. Ask these questions of the people you work with and your questions will move them. Things will be different just because you asked. Your questions stir the four key elements. Through questions and answers, the four elements are connected and the change dynamic begins.

This book revolves around the GTD model, with chapters highlighting one of the four key elements or the dynamics among them. The table of contents can guide you to particular elements or dynamics that interest you.

AN EXERCISE

Drawing Your Life

Deepen your familiarity with the GTD model by spending 15 minutes on these six steps.

1. Draw the four key elements of GTD model on a large sheet of paper. Make the circles large enough (3–4 inches across) that you can write or draw in them. Put the labels (WANTS, REALITY, PEOPLE, and YOU) above their circles.

2. In the REALITY, use words and symbols to represent your life as it is right now. That's right, your life. Indicate those parts of it that really stand out for you at the moment. Take just 2–3 minutes to do this.

3. In the WANTS circle, represent your life as you want it to be. With words or symbols note what you hope to have as a part of your future. It may include some of what you already have; it may include more. Take 2–3 minutes to do this.

4. In the PEOPLE circle, name people particularly important to you in your life—as it really is and/or as you want it to be. Note those people's names or roles or positions. Take a minute to do that.

5. In the YOU circle, note your reactions to the idea of engaging those PEOPLE in helping you move from the REALITY you've got toward what you WANT from your life. Spend 3–5 minutes thinking about yourself and making a few notes.

6. An option: Using this sheet as a visual aid, tell your friend, spouse, child, or parent about your life as you see it right now.

This exercise can form a deeper awareness of the GTD model and the dynamics within it. You can see, and perhaps feel, the differences between *reality* and *wants*; you imagine how these people affect the life you lead; you think about what you might do to get people's help. Most of the time in this book, we will be applying portions of the model to situations that are a subset of your life—particularly the work you are doing with others.

What to Read Next

The Getting Things Done model is the framework for the book. The chapters cover the model in this way:

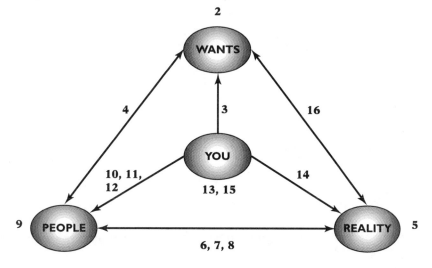

Each chapter focuses on a particular corner or connection of the model and has a central theme represented in the title of the chapter. The themes are sometimes questions (What is really important?) and sometimes direction (Face the politics). These are key questions and actions for you, the reader, to consider as you think about getting things done at work. Let's elaborate a bit more on the chapters surrounding the four main elements or corners of the model.

WANTS: "Why Is That Important?" To learn more about the importance of people's WANTS as related to leading and changing in your organization, begin with Chapter 2: Why Is That Important?; Chapter 3: Pursuing Your Aspirations; and Chapter 4: Discovering Dreams. WANTS draw us toward something better; WANTS cause movement. Without WANTS, nothing happens. Connect with their WANTS.

REALITY: "What Is Really Happening?" For more about assessing and understanding what is *really* going on right now, turn to Chapter 5: What Is Really Happening?; and Chapter 6: Build Common Understanding. We often miss out on the change we want because we are starting from different understandings of the current REALITY—what we have. If you want to succeed in getting things done with others, you'd better pay attention to their starting point.

PEOPLE: "Who Makes a Difference?"
If you want to learn about identifying and working with those people particularly important to the issues now facing you and the organization, try Chapter 9: Who Makes A Difference?; and Chapter 10: Enlist Able Partners. All the change we undertake comes through working with key people; these chapters focus on building constructive relationships with them.

YOU: "How Might You Help?"
If you want to learn more about yourself as a unique resource, begin with Chapter 13: How Might You Help?; Chapter 14: Find the Courage to Risk; and Chapter 15: Making Your Work Rewarding. All change starts here, whether we are aware of it or not. Our challenge is to become more aware and do our own work before we set out to do other people's work.

The first chapter of the book, and the last two, offer ideas and actions important to the entire GTD model. You have already read Chapter 1: A Model For Getting Things Done. Chapter 16: Create Change, lays out some of the ground rules for making change work, whether in your whole organization, your work group, or your own life. Chapter 17: Actions That Get Things Done, offers twenty ways I have used many times to stimulate some movement in an organization.

CHAPTER TWO

Why Is That Important?

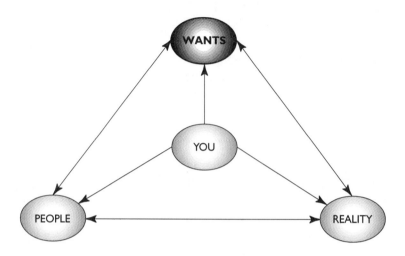

When attempting to move people from where they are right now toward something else, we often ask what is important to them? Good question, but I think not the *core* question. Ask them what and they will tell you the object, the person, the destination, the goal. That's helpful, but it stands in front of what they want even more deeply, does not reach for the source of the motivation. We know what they want, but why? For example, teenagers often want cars. What they want is pretty clear: a car. But why? Recognition, independence, excitement, freedom, fulfillment, attractiveness, friends—these are the whys behind the goal of car; these are continuing sources of motivation for these kids, whether they have a car or not.

And, when you want to help people in your workplace move from their current reality, you need to appeal to the whys behind their goals. Sure, talk with them about what they want, but more important, find out why they aspire to that goal. "Why is that important?" calls forth the deeper reasons and feelings behind the goal. Responses to the *what* question elicit concrete, material, short-term goals; the *why* question yields the heartfelt convictions and values that support the more tangible goals in life.

The top of the GTD model, the WANTS, are an essential element of change. PEOPLE value more than the current REALITY in which they live; they have WANTS that pull them toward somewhere, something, else. These WANTS provide motivation to change—their motive for action. Their WANTS are full of expectations, hopes, aspirations, values, even dreams. The WANTS provide the attraction that causes us to build plans. Escaping the present REALITY does not provide enough constructive direction; running anywhere is not the same as running somewhere. Our WANTS give us direction. Whether we are talking about our dreams for our children, or our hopes for our neighborhood, or intent for our monthly civic club meeting, the shared sense of what we want together adds a vital, positive spark to our work.

Many of us are conditioned to a problem-solving approach to the world. We journey along our work and life path, exerting extra effort when a problem comes our way. Then we figure out what's wrong and, hopefully, fix it, allowing us to return to our "normal" path. Well, that is a bit simple for those of us who journey from problem to problem and seem to live in the fix-it mode. But whatever our pace and intensity, if our patterned response is fix it, we are missing the perspective and potential that can come with lifting our heads to look at what we want. Leading from the bottom, middle, or top of organizations is about helping others lift their heads toward what they want and then moving together in that direction.

Our wants can be as simple as "I want to leave this retreat feeling a lot better about what we are doing together" or "I want to find three of you who will help me with this project." Or, as grand as "I want our community to be nationally recognized for our environmental accomplishment" or "I want us to know that we have contributed to world peace." The essential point with wants is not their reasonableness or their measurability; it is their magnetism. To work, they must draw people forward together.

The peak of the GTD model is not about what is right or correct; it is not about what others think we should want; nor is it about what we *think* we should want. It is about what we *want*, and to find out we have to ask. Hidden wants mean hidden motivation and hidden yearnings. The link between WANTS and life meaning is strong. Just as you can clarify what you want as you pursue your life, so can a small group discuss their group life purpose together; and, so can a school or a company or a foundation. Together they can decide on the future they want to create.

The title and content of this book links to life meaning—whether it's a person, a council, or a not-for-profit organization. It is about *getting work done and making meaning at the same time*. Years ago, these considerations were unusual in the organization world. Now business journals and books write about *ideals, purpose, meaning, hopes, vision,* and *dreams*. The number of inspiring and aspiring bestsellers to supposedly hard-nosed business people indicates we are recognizing the energy and action that come with clarity about wants. We must continue to keep one eye on what we have and the other eye on what we want and its importance to us.

Let's look at some of the big-picture categories within which people's wants might fall:

Dreams	Values	Meaning
Fantasies	Principles	Ideals
Visions	Accomplishments	Aspirations
Life goals	Mission	Higher purposes

These wants are on the hopeful and ambitious end of the spectrum. Achieving them may take years. Many of them—though never fully realized—will be guiding stars through life. They have counterparts at work, but they are best thought of in life terms, as in "These are my dreams/goals/aspirations for my life." This is what we are really reaching for, this is what all of our work dreams/goals/aspirations serve. Compelling, almost magnetic, forces draw us toward these grand wants. This is what we want most out of life; all of our daily actions (guided and misguided) point toward the fulfillment of these larger dreams. Although we may be focused on buying a house or finding a partner, our dreams are in play. The object of our immediate attention might be a promotion or a project, but something larger stands behind our effort. Whatever we do is in some way in service to what is deeply important in life. The pursuit of these grand wants makes our lives meaningful. You can help others in that pursuit. Discover what they want, why it is important, and what you could do together to move in that direction.

What Is Important

To get a deeper sense of your wants and their importance to you, take 10 minutes to write answers to these questions:

1. What do you do? Answer this question in one sentence.

2. Why is that important to you? Answer this question in one simple sentence.

3. And . . . Why is *that* important to you? Again, answer this question in one simple sentence.

4. And . . . Why is *that* important to you? Again, a simple sentence.

5. Look at your series of answers, each pursuing at a greater depth the answer to the previous question: In what direction are your answers leading? Are they pointing to anything? How would you describe the destination they are leading to? Write down a few words describing that destination.

6. Finally, what does this destination have to do with the reasons you do what you do? In other words, link back to the opening question in number 1.

Optional: Ask a friend or associate to answer the same series of questions—before you show your answers to them. Then compare your answers and talk about them.

Many people who have been through this exercise find their answers lead in the direction of deeper meaning, soul, purpose, values, and heart. Through the series of questions they consider the roots of why they do what they do. The questions lead them in the direction of what is truly important to them. They may not get there in these few questions, but they are pointed in that direction.

---

*Based on an exercise in *Your Signature Path: Gaining New Perspectives On Life and Work* by Geoff Bellman, Berrett-Koehler, 1996.)

When people compare answers with others, they usually find that the same questions lead them toward the same place. It's at the level of the third or fourth or even sixth *why* that they discover their connection with others. This is what they want together. Getting things done requires discovering what people want together. The united wants—explicit or implicit—provide the shared motivation to really do something significant. Without it, people are just going through the motions. And that is why wants are at the top of the GTD model.

CHAPTER THREE

Pursuing Your Aspirations

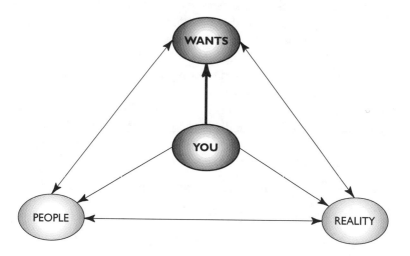

There YOU are, surrounded by the WANTS, the REALITY, and the PEOPLE in your organization. You are considering what you WANT the organization to do, what you WANT others to do, what you WANT to do together. Before moving others, you must move yourself. You must have clarity about what you want, your ability to put your wants forth, and your willingness to do so. We will step into the shaded portions of the GTD model as we consider:

- How can you discover and express your WANTS?

- What do you need to learn how to do to bring WANTS to life for yourself?

- What can you do with WANTS to support change in your organization?

The way to success in your work is to pursue and affirm what you want out of your life. This requires much more clarity about your life and wants than your organization usually asks of you. The organization's game is usually confined to what it wants and how you might help it get there. That is well and good, but it is not necessarily the way to build your investment or power. Define yourself, define your wants, and make the organization game a subset of your life game.

Know What You Want

If this were as obvious as it appears, we would acknowledge it more often. Too often we run off it the direction of what we *feel* we want before putting more thought behind it. Knowing what you want will serve you as you attempt to get things done: It will help you be clear with yourself, focusing your time and energy. It will help you be clear with others; you will be more compelling, more powerful with them. Others will know what they are signing up for; you will have clearer agreements with them and be more likely to be able to count on them.

Wants come in many shapes and sizes. Here are some you may have seen in your life:

- "I want to the organization to support this project."
- "I want to improve our board meetings."
- "I want this agency to better serve its clients."
- "I want people to feel good about living in our town."
- "I want us to have a party after our meeting on Friday!"
- "I want to feel better about working on this team."
- "I want to have a real life outside of work."

The time frames on fulfilling these wants vary from "can do now" to decades of work. The task anticipated varies from minimal to monumental. Your clarity about what you want, and are willing to take on, shapes what happens after you initiate action.

Know *Why* You Want What You Want

The "What Is Important?" exercise on page 14 explored the deeper meaning behind the work you do. If you didn't complete it then, do so now. Each of us shows up at work for very complicated reasons. We know what we do, when to do it and where; we usually know how. The big question of *why*—asked in that earlier exercise—often slips by unasked. Many of us do our work without thinking about the deeper whys. That is fine, unless you are unhappy about your work, or how you are treated, or the results your work group is getting, and you want some changes. Then the whys become very important, and they are linked to what you want.

As the GTD model shows, change takes place when PEOPLE take responsibility for the current REALITY and help move it toward their WANTS. Since you are going to be helpful in this, you need to be able to discover your wants and express them well. When you can do this with yourself, you are ready to begin to do it with others.

Your success at work is anchored in your personal vision and values. With everyone else's problems and priorities constantly pounding you, you will be successful to the extent that you know what you are trying to build and how you want to build it. Your *vision* is your picture of the possible future you want to build; your *values* are the beliefs that underlie your thoughts, words, feelings, and actions. There is nothing more useful in sorting out the tangle of daily business than clearly knowing what you want. You lead yourself through your life, and your work is a considerable part of that life. Making it all work together comes down to questions like this: If your *life* went especially well, what would you be experiencing and becoming 10 years from now? If your *work* went especially well, what would you be experiencing and becoming in 10 years? What have you done recently to bring this 10-year picture into being? We answer these questions by the actions we take today. Whether we are aware of what we want or not, today's actions shape our futures. We are moving, but what are we moving toward? We can be thoughtful and intentional in pursuit of what we want.

Wants Are Linked to Life Purpose

Wants unconnected to life purpose are not that important. The way you build power in your life and the organizations you work with is through a direct link between your wants and your life purpose. When that exists, you will take action because it is important to your life, not just because your current role requires it. For example, imagine two cancer-research scientists working side by side. One of them accepted the job because it was the highest salary offered when she graduated. The other took the job because of her desire to find a cure for cancer.

Now, imagine the daily decisions these two scientists must make about paths to pursue, effort to extend, hours to work, and information to share. The different considerations going through their brains probably result in different decisions. The way they individually use their power will be related to their pursuit of purpose.

What applies to our two scientists applies to everyone; we all have life purpose. Your starting point for significant change in your organization is hidden in various individuals' sense of purpose. Your path to helping reform your workplace goes through their lives, not just through their jobs. Find their larger life purpose that your WANT could fulfill and you are more likely to enlist them in reaching that goal.

Alignment of Wants Builds Power

When you and the organization want the same thing and know it, you are in a more powerful position than when you want something different from the organization. This is not to suggest that you should align yourself with the organization if you are not truly aligned. Do not do that. Instead, live with the consequences of not being aligned; do not waste energy cursing it. Accept this as an understandable outcome, considering you want different things.

Every place you find alignment between what you and others want strengthens your ability to get things done. Everywhere there is a gap, or you are at cross purposes, decreases your power. This is the truth. Do not fight it; learn from it while living with it.

Figure Out What You Want
Before Talking About It

Much of our confused expression, or lack of expression, comes from not knowing what we want in the first place. When we have thought about it and know, we will be more articulate. We have all been in meetings in which someone struggled to express something that they thought they wanted. We know the confusion we felt as we tried to understand what they were saying. There's a good chance that their confusion came from their own lack of clarity about what they wanted. That is not the way to get things done when you are not in charge. Better, seek clarity about what you want at a deeper level.

Each Day Remind Yourself What Is Important

One of the great things about work is its purposefulness. Everybody is busy doing something, going somewhere. But there is also a downside to all this busy-ness. That side says "Get something done *today*. Don't worry about tomorrow. Keep your nose to the grindstone." The net result is a work setting that encourages people to look and act purposeful but not worry about their purpose.

Common questions buzzing through our heads on a busy day include: What's next? What do I do now? In what order? By what time? How am I going to do everything? For whom? By when? Can I get there? The pressures of this first decade of the twenty-first century are phenomenally greater than even a decade ago, so the internal questions come at an even faster rate, crowding out our wants. Considering what we do want to do has become almost irrelevant. Yet, that is exactly where we must go if we are to get things done when we are not in charge.

Look at your calendar. What are you doing tomorrow? Of all that you've *got* to do, what do you *want* to do? Notice those commitments that you have for the next week. Which are important to you—not because you will be in trouble if you do not fulfill them, but because they excite you and you want to do them. We all need energy-generating work. Without regular exposure to it, your energy will be drained. Find a way to include something of what you want in each day. Some days, it might only be 15 minutes, but put something on your calendar every day. See what a difference it makes to be doing some of what you really want to do versus just what you have to do.

Lead Your Own Life

When we are not doing what we want to do, we are doing what others want us to do. That's not a criticism of them or what they are having us do, but it doesn't make for much change or excitement in our work. And it does make for passivity and reduced awareness. It's hard to lead your life by turning it over to someone else. It's hard to get what you want by expecting someone else to take care of it. How do you get what you want, except by luck, if you do not engage? Don't leave your life for someone else to examine and use. Examine it yourself. Pursue it yourself.

Immediate Fulfillment
Requires Immediate Action

"I want to have a party after our meeting on Friday!" This example of a want has a short time fuse, elicits a quick response from a limited number of others, and quickly shifts to action: Who is going to bring what food, and where? As the initiator, you must be tactical, willing to help put your want into action when others accept it. People know what a party is, they know it is likely to be fun, they know what their calendars look like. They are ready to make this low-risk decision involving only a few people. When you get support for your want, you had better be ready to help shape logistics. Have this in mind when you put your want forth. Contrast the immediate fulfillment of this want with longer-term WANTS.

Distant Fulfillment Requires Persistence

"I want people to feel good about living in our town." What is the time frame for fulfillment of this want? Two years? Ten? Twenty? Imagine the consistent attention required all across town to deliver on this want. As the initiator of this want, you must be quite visionary and strategic; you need to be ready to engage many people in envisioning of what kind of town they want. You and others will have to return to the residents again and again, year after year, reminding them of the town that they aspire to have together. When you and others begin, this is at the level of a dream, and forming the same dream in each citizen is a huge challenge. Know this well ahead of time, because people will immediately sense the vastness of the task and may oppose it on that basis alone.

The two above wants contrast in concreteness-abstractness, time frame, specificity, risk, and number of people involved. When voiced, these two wants lead the initiator down quite different paths. Be ready to deal with what you are starting. This book will help.

Know *How* You Want to Work with Others

Expressing a want is not just about *what* you want; it's also about *how* you will get it. If you were talking with friends or co-workers about how you want to work with others, what would you say? What do you particularly value in your work relationships with others? If you were to give your three best answers, what would they be? Think about this for a few minutes and make a few notes to yourself.

Here are some of my own work values that are reflected in this book. I try to pay attention to them as I work with others. Finding them draws me closer to the work; their absence causes me to pull away. You can see how they fit with your own.

1. *Balance.* My work is in service to my larger life.

2. *Innovation.* My work feeds my need to grow and create.

3. *Authenticity.* Most often, my work encourages me to be myself rather than to play a role.

4. *Contribution.* Through my work, I make a small but positive difference in the community.

5. *Courage.* I am willing to risk my standing with others to support ideas and actions.

6. *Quality.* My work standards are high; I hold myself to them.

7. *Fairness.* I judge people on their potential contribution to and investment in our work together.

8. *Trust.* I will deal with others openly and positively, and assume I can count on them and they on me.

Work values like these have implications for how work proceeds. People will be drawn to or repelled by your work values. When projects go awry, most of the time it is because people differ on how to approach the work, not because they differ on what the work is. Whether paid work or volunteer work or work around the house, you have work values that you carry from place to place. Know what your work values are and learn what others' values are; make this a subject of discussion, not an assumption. Express your work values early—as you begin partnering with others. This will affect both the work you do and how you talk about it.

For the lone reader trying to figure out whether to speak up on an issue in tomorrow's staff meeting, this section on work values may seem far afield, but it is not. All our work values cannot be fulfilled in one staff meeting, but our values provide the substance behind each specific action. Holding the value of *courage* can be what allows you to speak up in tomorrow's meeting. Lacking *courage* feeds silence.

Figuring out how you want to work with others anticipates and eliminates smaller daily difficulties. When you know what you want, many decisions make themselves.

CHAPTER FOUR

Discovering Dreams

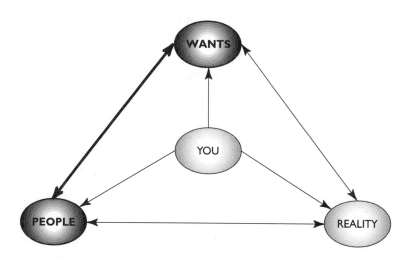

Established WANTS anchor the top corner of the GTD model. The clearer the WANTS, the more specific you can be about the gap between the WANTS and REALITY. And, clear WANTS tell us about the motivation and energy available to us in the key PEOPLE. The previous chapter helped you imagine what you want and value, a good step before attempting to move your organization. Next, begin involving others in the same process; you need to know what they want—especially what they want that you also want. Your focus, and the primary focus of this chapter, is helping others discover what they want.

Wants Always Exist

Here is a sampling of wants collected from group meetings in an Internet company. When asked what they want, people said:

Stock options

A more motivated work team

To get along better with the boss

Lifelong happiness

To reduce the scrap rate	To make a plan this month
A sabbatical	To be proud of their work
To leave this meeting early	To cut back to a 70-hour week
More flexible work hours	To raise healthy children
A computer at home	To celebrate work successes
A cold beer	An online training program
To clean up their paperwork	

I offer this diverse array of wants so you will think about what is going on in the minds and hearts of the people with whom you work. A similarly diverse array faces you when you begin your work of aligning what your key people want. They are wondering and weighing what you might be offering against what they want. "How will this help me get what I want?" is the question on their minds. Their wants, and their self-serving question, deserve your respect.

If you have never asked people what they want, your initial reaction to their responses might be to resolve never to do it again. People have so many different wants that to hear them can be overwhelming. Whether you ask or not, the wants are there, waiting to be expressed. When you don't ask, you condemn yourself to ignorance and guessing. When you do ask, people express what is important to them in their work and lives; this is information you can use. When you do not ask, you will not know.

When you ask, people usually appreciate it. They usually don't say "Wow, thanks, you are terrific!" They show their appreciation through the enthusiasm they bring to their responses. Even an angry person who rants on is saying, at one level, "I value this opportunity to say what is on my mind. That's why I am talking like this, letting off steam. It's nice to know that someone cares what I think and feel." And you, of course, reinforce this thought by telling people, showing them, that you appreciate hearing from them. You tell them what you've heard; you check to make sure that you understand. You restate what they have said in your own words. All of this helps them know that they are getting through to you.

What happens when people express wants that cannot be met? Whether their wants can be met or not, people still have them. Whether you ask them or not, they are going to compare your wants to their wants and decide how much they will cooperate. Understanding their wants is valuable information for you, helping you to assess the possibility of bringing about change.

Express the Dream

Do it yourself and help others do it. Reaching for a better day or better work or a better life requires that people talk about it. And they must express much more than what they know about the REALITY that faces them today; they must talk about the new reality they want. This is a little risky for people because maybe this new reality will never come about. True, but if they never talk about it, they will not know what they want to do together. Dreams, hopes, fantasies, and visions draw us forward—whether we want to acknowledge them or not. Your challenge is to find ways to get people to dream together. Not about what they want next week, but what they want next year and beyond.

Nowadays many organizations have prepared written vision, values, or mission statements. This is not a bad place to start. Though often these statements are not widely endorsed by workers, they legitimize the function of organizational dreaming. The written statement can be a good backboard off of which a group can bounce their ideas. If your organization has not developed a vision statement, start by asking questions related to the future people want and why that is important to them. You are not looking for sophisticated responses, but honest responses. When you hear people speak about what they want, their responses suggest where their energy lies and how you might draw on that energy.

Discover What They Want That You Want

Start with the assumption that there is something that they want that you also want; it is just a matter of discovering what your common wants are and how immediate they are to the present situation. The closer the wants are to what faces all of you today, the better. For example, if you need a little help budgeting right now, and I have the skills, time, and desire to help, our immediate wants overlap. We will come to quick agreement and go to work. On the other hand, if you are behind schedule in production, and I need your budget yesterday, our common wants are not as evident and overlapping in the immediate situation facing us. This makes our work together more difficult.

Successful working relationships depend on discovering *now* what you and others want together. For example, when you and I resolve a pressing issue together now, an issue we both care about now, that breeds success. Or, in the example above—when I provided you with a little budgeting help—that also fits the bill: It is mutual and immediate; we are both invested. At the other end of the spectrum are the most difficult problems—the ones where you can find nothing that you both want from the present situation, and neither can you find anything in the organization that you both want. Then you have to appeal to mutual life values like success, growth, happiness, and strength to join the people involved. It is quite a reach to bring two people together with only these personal wants and values in common, but it is still a starting point. Consider:

- What do I want?

- What do they want?

- What do our wants have in common?

- Which of these wants might be met immediately through working together?

- How can I help us realize our common wants?

Build Commitment to Wants

One "secret" to getting things done is helping people to discover what they really want. All of us can get so caught up in doing our work that we lose track of what we really want. Help others think about what they really want to accomplish through their work. A second "secret" is to enlist people's commitment to what they want. Discovering and becoming clear about what you want does not automatically move you to action. For example: I want to lose weight and I am doing absolutely nothing about it. Lately, I've just been so busy—I do want to lose weight, but not just now. If I *committed* to being healthier and thinner, that would be significantly different. Commitment moves me past a more neutral understanding of what I want to doing something about it. Commitment is taking responsibility for building what we want.

Reinvent the Wheel

"Let's not reinvent the wheel." How many times have you heard that? I am here to argue that we *must* reinvent the wheel. Despite the caution, we reinvent wheels regularly and successfully. I am not arguing that it's necessary every time, but most of what we do involves reinventing something that has been done before. Most of what we do in our lives has been done before by somebody else. Our parents were very good at reminding us of this, and we are almost as good at reminding our own children. This is equally true in organizations. Those who do not learn from history (past wheels) are doomed to repeat it. We repeat history because, although it has been done before, *we did not do it*. And *we* want to, need to, do it ourselves in order to believe it, to commit to it, to take pride in it. We want to do it ourselves so that we will know what it is like at a personal level.

Why did we reinvent a capital assets system that is available from our accountant? Why did we build an orientation program for our area instead of using the one that headquarters provides? Why did we design our own website when we could have borrowed the design of a neighboring region with much less effort? Why? Because we want to do it ourselves, we want to own it, we want to be committed to it, we want to believe in it, we want to be proud of it, we want to say "We did this! This is our wheel!" Besides, we really don't understand how and why it works until we have done it ourselves.

Now let's shift our focus to your work. Imagine that you are about to propose a new program (or system or procedure or structure) for your organization that would replace an existing one. Imagine that what you are proposing has been very successful in many organizations similar to yours. People here will love it—once it is in place. But do they believe this? Do they trust your recommendations? Do they accept the successful experiences of others? No, no, and no. So, what do you do? If you are smart, you reinvent the wheel. You know that the new program is not all you are working with here. You know that you need the support of real people, with real energy that they can use for or against it. So you spend hours helping people look at their wants and needs. You involve all the key people who could be involved with the new program. You attend to their needs for special tailoring to their unique situation. And this isn't whitewash; you really do pay attention. You look forward to the day when they say "This is our system; we built it the way we wanted it." The program needs commitment over the long term and you get that by engaging the group in reinventing the wheel.

Help Them Know That You Know

We often act like we "know" what is going on. We tell others that we know; we want them to know that we understand. And, often we are wrong. I am trying to learn from experiences like this one: I was telling a group of directors about the problems they had working with the divisions of the organization. I said that I knew how this bothered them and knew what they could do about it. Fortunately, early inquiries from the group revealed that they did not want to hear my opinions on what they wanted and needed. They preferred to tell me about the difficulties they were having adjusting to a recent merger with another organization. That was the pain they wanted to deal with right then. My opinions about problems with their divisions were not relevant at this moment. I could have tried to convince them that we should talk about my agenda and that would have failed. We did what they wanted to do, and that worked.

It is not enough for you to know what they want: They must know that you know. When they do, they are ready to move forward. When others think you do not understand what they want, they will move only with great reluctance. The frustration caused by a problem—or the enthusiasm generated by an opportunity—releases energy and allows people to lean into action. When you propose action steps before these feelings are expressed, you are likely to get resistance. People will not be ready to move into solutions until they have expressed their feelings about the situation as it exists now and how it differs from what they want. It is common for groups to have a general, loose agreement about what they want but to disagree strongly about what should be done to move toward this common want. The agreement is the part to focus on. You can only help your group move forward in areas where they agree. Unresolved disagreements within the group pull them and dissipate the energy needed to move to action.

Collaboration and Negotiation: Your Best Options

Working with people often comes down to one of three situations: (1) You have the same wants, (2) you have different wants, or (3) both are true. Same wants call for *collaboration*: "When we work together, we will get what we both want." Different wants call for *negotiation*: "I'll help you get what you want; you help me get what I want." A mix of different or overlapping wants calls for a *combined tactic*: "Let's work toward this goal together because we both want it, and then we can support each other on what we each want that is different."

Each position calls for you to be clear about what you want from the people with whom you are working. You expect the same clarity from them. Expect toe-to-toe encounters. Expect some searching for higher ground. Expect candor. Expect to work hard to get what you want and they want. It's not easy to be truly collaborative or to negotiate openly.

Competition and Avoidance: Not Your Best Options

In your search for shared wants, you don't have to collaborate or negotiate; you can compete or avoid. But these latter two tactics do not regularly work well for people who are not in charge. Perhaps for someone else, but not for you. Consider the competitive approach: "We both want the same thing; only one of us can have it." We are all familiar with this option, but how well does it work for you? Competing and winning over others is not the way to gain their support. Consider, are you prepared to compete? What do you have in your arsenal? How well does your position in the organization prepare you to compete? What if they win? Consider the consequences for you, the others, and the organization; you will likely move on to other tactics.

A fourth tactic is to avoid the people and the issue altogether. This gains you temporary protection, but seldom progress. Important differences in wants between others and yourself must be faced for the sake of your own effectiveness. The issue will have to be dealt with; you cannot count on its going away. Yes, avoiding can be a legitimate tactic— you just need to consider the consequences. Usually avoidance does not contribute to your power in the organization.

CHAPTER FIVE

What Is Really Happening?

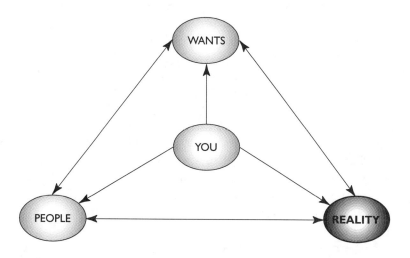

REALITY is the mucky ground you walk on, run across, skip through, and slip in each day of your life. Whether at home or at work, REALITY is always there demanding your attention. Whatever we get done happens in the present, the now, the current REALITY. If we have any hope of engaging others in changing the places we work, we have to work with them in the present; we have to discover our shared sense of what is real now. And if we want to appeal to our more pragmatic colleagues, we have to speak to them in terms of what is going on now. We first have to agree upon what is really happening before we can move forward together. So that is the key question of this chapter: What is really happening?

Often, we get so caught up in REALITY, we begin to doubt there is anything else. Witness your coworkers (or yourself) defining the work world as the entire world. Notice people with no tolerance for other world views, or those who cannot stand "dreamers." These distortions on REALITY make it central and compelling. Any larger life energy is captured in the immediate focus on work. This corner of the GTD model is our anchor in the "real world" while we reach for our WANTS.

REALITY is confusing and chaotic—and captivating. Befuddling and bewildering—and bewitching. This is where our dreams begin to come to life.

We distinguish ourselves in life and work when we can reach for the stars and keep our feet on the ground *at the same time.* Our most successful accomplishments usually involve both. Launching ourselves starry-eyed into idealistic visions, or, burying ourselves deep in the ground of current reality—these are polar alternatives, each incomplete without some of the other. We may be tempted to forego reality for the dream, but understanding REALITY allows the first steps that make dreams possible. We may be tempted to forego the dream for the REALITY, but over time, that yields stale results and uneasy yearnings.

Helping people express what they want, together, is often easier than getting them to agree on what they've got. The WANTS are by definition above the current REALITY. The encouragement to dream a little lifts people above their daily concerns to their notions of a better world. That world is often filled with fairness, truth, beauty, justice, charity, and goodness. PEOPLE can agree that they WANT this together. Getting agreement on what they currently have, REALITY, is another matter. They often hold up quite separate pictures about what is happening now, who is responsible, the key issues, and what might be done. Despite the fact that they work closely with each other, sometimes even in the same work space, they take markedly different pictures of it. The challenge is to help them hear each other's reality for the sake of building a common REALITY. Chapters 6 and 7 discuss some the practical aspects of doing this.

Five Steps to Discovering Reality

We gather information through our five senses so we can decide what to do next. Whether we are looking for the latest social trends or the restroom, we each have an underlying process. And our processes differ from person to person. Consider this five-step approach for discovering what is going on and acting on it.

Step One: Identify Issue. First, we become uncomfortable with what is going on right now; we sense there is a difference between what is happening and what we want. It may be that our work is taking us in a direction we do not like. Or, it begins to rain as we start out on a long walk. Or, the stock market is doing much better than anticipated. In

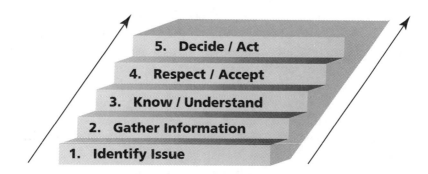

each of these situations, we sense a discomfort and consider action within our minds and bodies. We each have our own sensors and our own process for dealing with what we learn from the world around us. What is an issue for me may not be an issue for you. So the next three steps are especially important in this reality-discovering process.

Step Two: Gather Information. Before taking action, we can find out more. We can ask others, study the issue, take in relevant data. We may do this at some distance, almost like laboratory research, learning without disturbing what is going on. Or, we may dive right in, asking questions of people key to the issue, reading files, calling meetings. In any number of ways, we attempt to find out more. This makes so much sense that pointing it out may seem superfluous. But recall the times that you have seen yourself or others jump into action without gathering more information. And without valuable, available information, the next two steps just will not happen.

Step Three: Know/Understand. It is one thing to gather the information and quite another to understand it. Knowledge comes from familiarizing yourself with the data and information gathered. It is not enough to say, "I have read the report" or "We have all the data we need." Understanding moves beyond knowledge. The ability to recite the data is not as important as interrelating it, making whole meaning that goes beyond the parts. One clue that you have understanding is when knowledgeable others *say* you understand. In fact, a useful goal is to reach the point where others say "She really knows what we are talking about" or "He has developed a deep sense of what we are struggling with here." This level of understanding moves you to the possibility of Step Four.

Step Four: Respect/Accept. When you are at this step, you know, understand, and appreciate what others have done. Respecting and accepting others does not necessarily mean agreement, and it most certainly does not include scoffing or deriding their work. You recognize that people's intentions are honorable, perhaps even noble, though not necessarily skillful or effective. What they have done, what has happened, can be respected. This is a difficult step to reach because it involves holding our wants at a distance while appreciating what *is* happening. When we can reach this level, we form deeper bonds with those involved, and they are more likely to see us as trustworthy. Though it is not essential that we reach this level to assist change, we have more of an uphill fight without it.

In an accepting mode, you might say something like this to a group: "I know a lot about this department that I didn't know a few weeks ago. I think I understand what you have had to deal with; many of you have told me that I really do understand. I respect your hard work; I respect the talent you have poured into making this department run. I also accept that the people in this department are smart, hardworking, interested in contributing, and valuable to the company. I love working with you, and I look forward to our work together." All of that can be true, and you may still disagree with what they have been doing. Acceptance means grasping the situation in a way that is not condemning of the people involved in it. Acceptance does not mean acquiescence or agreement.

Step Five: Decide/Act. After all of your data gathering, understanding, respecting, and accepting, it's time to decide what to do. Some of us are pretty good at this step; we look at our options and we pick from what has come to us in earlier steps.

The better we know, understand, respect, and accept reality together, the better we can move toward our collective wants. We won't get there by fooling ourselves about our starting reality. Denying reality seldom proves a constructive step. When we already have one foot in the air, stretching toward our wants, we don't need our other foot in the air too! The five steps we just walked through lead toward a discovery of the truth. Discovering the truth is a learning process. See yourself as a student more than as a detective. You are not solving a crime and placing blame. You are a curious student trying to understand how things work. You want the whole truth, not just the good news or the bad news.

Organizational Reality

Consider how problems are typically approached and solved in your organization.

1. *Use your experience to describe what usually happens when a problem appears.* Who is brought together? When? Where? How do they typically deal with the problem? With the gap they want to close? How aware are they of how they solve problems? How successful are they in this process? Make notes on these questions.

2. *Put your thoughts and notes beside each of the five steps in the process* described earlier: What do they typically do to gain knowledge of the problem? How do they pursue deeper understanding of the problem? How do they demonstrate their acceptance of this real problem that faces them? Note the extent to which these five steps naturally emerge, or do not emerge, in your organization's typical approach. What do they leave out? What do they add in?

3. Based on what you have thought and noted so far—and compared to the five steps—*how well does your organization's current approach work? What might it do more effectively in the future?*

When I have asked others about their results from this exercise, the most frequent report is "In our organization, we do steps one and five—usually in that order. And sometimes we go for step two." See how that fits with your experience.

These five steps for discovering and acting on reality have many useful applications. For example, you could adapt the simple structure to pursuing a better work relationship with an associate. In the middle three steps, you might use questions and statements like these: "How would you describe how we work together? . . . Let me see if I understand you.

What you are saying is . . . Have I got it? . . . I appreciate your point of view. In fact, if I were in your shoes, I would see it the same way." Or, if you were dealing with a group that is trying to work better together, you might incorporate the five steps through phrases like these: "First, let's list some words and phrases that describe how we work together. Then we will go back through our list and mark all those that we agree upon. Okay? . . . As I look over our agreements about how we work together, it seems as if we are saying . . . How does that fit with your understanding? Are we all seeing this in the same way? . . . Have we developed a description of our working relationship that we all support? Can we all agree that this description accurately reflects the group's position—even though as individuals we may have said it differently?" The same thinking could be pursued with a larger organization. There are ways of knowing, understanding, and respecting for human organizations of all sizes. However we discover it, our shared sense of reality is our common starting point.

Love of the Bumps

One week a year, I strap long, expensive boards on my feet and slide down mountains. Occasionally I leave the safety of smooth, groomed runs to face the terror of the moguls. Moguls are big bumps of snow and ice formed on steep mountain slopes by large numbers of damned fools skiing back and forth, intent on killing themselves. When enough of them do this often enough, vertical football fields full of bumps emerge on mountainsides. Skiing them well requires strength, dexterity, foolhardiness, and knees possessed only by the young. Others try, and at the end of the day we gather to tell our stories about how we almost died that day. Yes, died! We love to tell how hard it was and how much we hurt as a result. If you do not ski and were to listen to us, you might think that our families are being held at gunpoint, only to be released after we ski these treacherous bumps at least ten more times. But you would be wrong. We choose to face the possibility of death and back braces. We do this on purpose! We love it! And we love to talk about how hard it is, how brave we are.

This short skiing story can be seen as a dramatic portrayal of the lives many of us live in organizations. Many of us love the organizational bumps. And we gather to tell stories of how brave we are, our risk of certain death, our saving of ourselves, our organizations, or our families. We would curl up and die without the daily challenges. We love to tell others about the bumps and mountains that we face, ascend, and ski down daily. We like to show off our ego's cuts and bruises to appreciative listeners. We love to tell of how close we came to organizational death. Listen to the pride and courage behind these expressions: "And you should have seen the look on their faces when I said that!". . . "He told me that, if he could, he'd fire me! But he couldn't!". . . "I had to work day and night to get it done.". . . "I was the first person to ever speak up to her in that way!". . . "I told them to go out and buy dinner, I was too busy to feed them!". . . "My tail was really on the line, but I delivered!" Those lines are from wonderful personal stories. They show the "bumps" as a critical element of our lives and our work. Our stories show how brave, how courageous, we are. And, sometimes, how foolish we are. And they show our deep engagement with the messy heart of reality.

For some of you life is a little too messy, a little *too* interesting right now. Yes, you can kill yourself on the bumps, whether they are in the Rockies or in the office. Have the sense to pull back; don't deeply injure yourself, mistaking foolishness for courage. And, for those of you who never love the bumps, they are optional; there are other paths down the mountain that can serve you just as well. Or, you can move to another mountain, get other work. Find the level of challenge you are looking for. Pick work that feeds your soul and doesn't just batter you. Your life is too important to waste on a job that punishes you with little hope of reward. Meaningful work can support a meaningful life. Seek some joy in the work you do each day.

CHAPTER SIX

Build Common Understanding

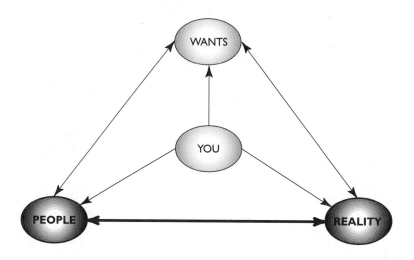

We have explored the importance of our WANTS to getting things done. These dreams pull us toward our better selves; they pull us from the present toward a finer future. But they cannot carry the entire change load. This chapter is about the other two corners of the GTD model and the connection between them. This chapter connects REALITY with the key PEOPLE. The directive "Build Common Understanding" tells you to help key PEOPLE develop a shared appreciation of what is going on right now. That's a role for you to focus on throughout the chapter. To oversimplify, before YOU come along, every person holds their separate understanding of what is going on right now. Your job is to get those individual perspectives out in the open so that people can decide what they know, feel, and believe together. Without help like yours, everyone may continue in their separate perspectives. You can see the opportunity.

It's a challenge to move people toward a common sense of "what is." If there are significant issues, many of them will be ready for action and not talk. As mucky as the current reality might be, it is still the base you move from as you step out together. It is the common ground we are anchored in and it can allow us to move forward. But, without the shared understanding, it will hold us back and consume valuable energy.

Much of the time people do not even try to build wide agreement among the involved parties. Often, they assume that others see the situation the same way they do. Or, that others are so far off base there is no point in talking with them. People play along, acting as if they all understand together. There is no harm in this if they do not need to do anything important together. When you speak up with your version of what is wrong around here, I am often silent even if I disagree. And when I speak up, you are silent. The result can be that we head off to solve different problems "together," thinking we are joined in our understanding. Now imagine expanding our lack of communication to 20 or 200 people, each with their own separate and, often, unexpressed views. This lack of a shared sense of reality weakens what we do together and makes us harder to move. Consider the Democratic and Republican parties. The Democratic party contains many and diverse groups in its base. The Republican party has generally been considered more homogeneous. The Democrats have a large challenge in building a common perception of reality across their many constituencies; as rich a tapestry as this might be, it is difficult to weave. The Republicans may be able to weave much more quickly but, some would say, with less color and varied creativity. There are consequences of each approach, but assembling a common reality has been much more difficult for the Democrats—except in regard to the opposite party!

Help Others Find and Face the Truth

This is more difficult than it sounds. Each of us carries a sense of what reality is and we are reluctant to let go of it. After all, we succeed moment to moment based on responding well to the world as we know it. When you suggest to me that there are other ways for me to see the world, I can easily hear you as saying that I do not know what I am doing. I will not let go easily.

On the other hand, much research suggests that one of the primary reasons people cannot solve their problems is because they have incorrectly described what is now going on. When they let go of their present understanding and find a different description, they often succeed in resolving the problem. My own experience suggests that, as much as 80 percent of the time, people are working on a misdiagnosed problem.

For example, a volunteer group of ten people ("The Ten") recently failed in their annual contribution drive, which supports their work in their community. The Ten got together to ask "What did we do wrong?" They had no difficulty listing a dozen mistakes they had made that contributed to their failure. But after completing the list and planning actions for next time, they still didn't feel any better. They were sure that if the listed actions were taken, things would work better, but their lingering discomfort suggested that the problem was still not solved—or that there was a deeper problem. Long conversation revealed that many of them were tired of the annual drive, tired of being one of The Ten, that this volunteer work no longer motivated them. This was the deeper reason behind the failures; this was closer to the real problem, closer to the truth, and required different action. The Ten explored the kinds of volunteer work that could be exciting for each of them, and this led to their reshaping both their work in the community and the way they sought funding for it. All ten signed up to carry out the new plan, and they began the new year with much more commitment to their work together. This example demonstrates an important truth: There are alternative ways of understanding reality. We need to search them out, because new understandings reveal new options.

The Organizational Village

Our organizations resemble country villages more than the collection of plans and strategies and results written about in annual reports. Yes, villages . . . Villages merging with other villages . . . Villages with people talking over back fences . . . Villages with richer and poorer citizens . . . Villages with front streets and back alleys. Like small towns, our organizations have:

Recorded history

Ritualized ways of dealing with events

Intelligence and resources

An established pace

Older and younger members

An idealized view of themselves

A cynical view of themselves

Aspirations and disappointments

If we are going to work successfully over years in these organizational villages, we must deal with all of the above. In fact, we *are* dealing with it—whether we are effective or not. That is the reality; we are a part of it. Anyone who tries to change the reality becomes a part of the reality. Changing it from the outside is an illusion.

We are closer to the reality of organizations when we think of them in this way—more like villages than machines. We have to accept them as they are, not pretend otherwise or insist that they should change. This is the primary challenge of this reality point of the GTD model. The secondary challenge is *agreeing together* on what they are.

Chapter 5 offered a five-step approach: Identify Issue, Gather Information, Know/Understand, Respect/Accept, Decide/Act. The middle three steps emphasized the deeper exploration that usually opens more options for action. Those steps also increase empathy and sympathy for people caught in the situation; we know at a deeper level what is going on; we are more in touch. In a way, as we gather information through the steps, we are nodding our heads and saying "Yes, I can see how this makes sense; I can see why people act as they do." This does not mean that we agree but that we understand. We can even understand how it can happen that many able people did their very best and are still caught in a situation that isn't working.

Building Understanding in Organizations

Listen in on these comments collected over coffee breaks at an urban social agency: ". . . and these people think they are *running* this place? They don't have a clue as to what is going on!" and "She must be crazy to make a decision like that!" or "He is so out of touch with reality!" and "They are making decisions from out in the void somewhere." Each of these statements—and many others you have heard—assume that someone who *thinks* they know what is going on *does not really know* what is going on. They are uninformed, maybe even crazy; we know that, and they do not. And, we are not going to tell them. The coffee break comments suggest there is no sense in what is being done, or at least that sense cannot be perceived.

Do you know where your organizations is going? Do you receive the guidance and information you need to act with confidence? If you do, you are the exception. If you do not, welcome to a large and not very exclusive club. Take a tour around the clubhouse; talk with some of the other members; you will hear comments like we heard in the agency. "Sometimes I wonder if we know where we are going". . . "One day she says this and the next day she says that". . . "Our committee is so divided on what is really important". . . "You can't count on him to hold a position". . . "Can't they see that the decision they made this morning flies in the face of what we have been doing for the last two years?" You can easily add a few of your own. It is easy for us to see the contradictory behavior of our organizations and the people who run them. If you have people working for you, they may be making similar comments about you.

It is not so much about facing reality as it is about discovering it *together*: From all that we know, does this make sense to everyone? Most of us are not crazy; most of us take action with reasons. It makes sense to us. The starting point for someone to move us individually is knowing where we begin. And the same is true for a group or a community or a country. The assumption that people take action because it makes sense to them influences the whole book, but especially these three chapters linking people and reality. From this perspective, hierarchy makes sense, authority makes sense, organizations make sense, even power and politics make sense. And that is the challenge in building a common understanding: To find out how the world makes sense to others and then to use that knowledge to bring them together.

CHAPTER SEVEN

Face the Politics

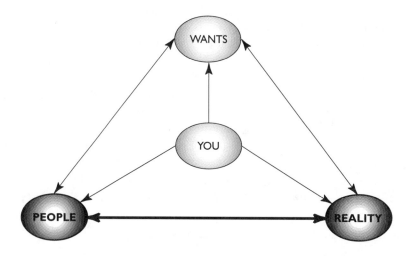

Company politics. Bridge club politics. Church politics. City politics. When you read *politics*, what words come to your mind? Quickly, come up with three. Chances are, the thoughts and feelings behind these three words reflect your first reactions to the politics that surround you at work. They shape the lens through which you see all interactions. They color the meaning you extract from actions you witness.

Review the words you noted a moment ago: Do they reflect a negative bias? If so, then this chapter is particularly for you—especially if you combine a distaste for politics with frustration about your ability to get things done in your organization. Like you, I have seen the downside of politics. I have observed actions that I saw as politically motivated. I have seen others celebrate the results of their clever political moves. And I have come up on the short end of organizational politics, seeing myself and my work put aside for political reasons. This has angered and hurt me, but in the process I learned a little.

A few years ago, I was asked to write an article on power and politics. In the process of writing, I interviewed six executives, all successful in their organizations. A common definition of *politics* emerged:

"The way we get things done around here." No, they did not each say exactly the same words, but they all agreed with the definition when they saw the article. So politics is about getting things done. These "in charge" people agreed, and all of us "not in charge" people should too. There is something about the idea of an organization without politics that disturbs, even chills, me. And, I have found much more success, much more to contribute, by moving *toward* the political dynamics than staying away from them.

Later in my employed career, I became director of a corporate department in a drug company. Before that move, I had been an internal consultant with an oil company. As a consultant, my emphasis was on achievement, completion of projects with quality results, and client satisfaction. I had great disdain for that oil company's political system and ran afoul of it a few times. I brought that bias to my new director position; I applied the talents that had worked well in my previous job and I built and managed a group of twenty people. I was working very hard with some—but limited—success.

After about six months, my boss sat me down for a "facts of life" discussion about the realities of working and contributing in this organization. He pointed out how very political it was—like it or not. He told me that he thought I was distancing myself from the political realities of the company, and that my department's effectiveness depended on my understanding how the company really worked. He was right on all counts. I was avoiding politics like the plague. My avoidance meant that I knew less about what was going on and even less about how to deal with it. This is not the way to get things done. This is not the way to be influential.

This wise mentor convinced me to begin to learn more about politics. At least I could get close enough that I could better understand the game—whether I decided to play or not. Yes, moving toward politics does risk "catching the disease." I risked losing my perspective and values. I risked being seduced by the political system. But increased political understanding also gave me more options. I knew more about what would likely work. I felt better prepared to get the results that I so wanted to deliver. Because of all that, I was more powerful.

Politics Are Real and Inescapable

Successful people recognize that politics are inescapable. Politics run through organizations of all sizes from families to villages to corporations to nations. They are not basically good or bad; they are neutral, to do with as we will. Political goodness or badness flows from the intent and impact of our actions. Politics result in trust and distrust, loyalty and undermining, giving and withholding, contacting and avoiding. Without the formal and informal political systems that exist in your organization, it would come to a halt. Or, maybe, because of the formal and informal political systems it has come to a halt. Either case demonstrates the power and importance of politics in your organization.

We are not going to be very effective if we ignore the politics of the organization, the "art of getting things done." Politics involves knowing who to work with and how to work with them. If you want to change the system, you had better understand how it works. You can try to avoid the politics of your organization, but you cannot stay outside of politics. It automatically includes you as a force whether you include yourself or not. Others make you a player even when you do not see yourself that way.

Some of our fears about politics come from the reality that it represents large and unknown powers outside our present understanding and control. There are no rulebooks about how to play the political games of your organization. It is unpleasant to be subject to rules you have yet to figure out. But to the extent that you can understand how the game is played, who makes the rules, and what your role is, you can make better decisions about your actions. This is where the organization game comes up against your life game. When there is a significant overlap, you can play in both games. When there is no overlap, the political game becomes intolerable and you have to step away from it physically, mentally, or emotionally. An underlying question is whether this is your kind of game, your kind of politics.

My Kind of Politics

Consider for a moment how you prefer people to work with each other. Here are a few statements gathered from others: "I want people to be open and above-board". . . "No talking behind each others' backs". . . "People should be heard based on what they can contribute, not based on their position". . . "When people have trouble with what I'm doing, I want them to tell me". . . "We should recognize people for their contributions". . . "When you request personal leave, your job level shouldn't make any difference". . . "Decisions should be in the hands of the people doing the work." These are all political statements. To the extent you agree with them, they are your political statements. Yes, the statements are slanted toward fairness, openness, and trust; but that's politics too. A significantly different variety, but politics nevertheless. We like our kind of politics.

What if we did away with politics? What difference would it make to you? It could mean losing the advance warning you get from a co-worker about the boss calling you on an issue. It could mean not being able to seek support for a proposal before taking it to a meeting. It could mean no more informal chats with the head of your organization about your future. Small actions like these lubricate the clunky wheels of cumbersome organizations. Politics fills the white space around the jobs on an organization chart. The real work gets done in that white space. This is where you decide, where you are influenced, build trust, take risks, and reveal who you really are.

Your Mix of Politics and Values

A good working environment is not achieved by removing politics, since we could not do this even if we wanted to. Instead, we need to recognize that we are participants in politics. We need to know the kind of political atmosphere we support and to do our part to bring it to reality. Given that this is such a difficult area for many of us, how can you be true to yourself *and* get things done in your organization?

- *Accept the reality of politics.* Do not waste much time cursing the political realities. Accept that politics are a legitimate organizational force and seek to understand them. Test your understanding on others; hear their political views.

- *You are a player in the political process.* You cannot declare yourself out because others will not let you. You may not be playing in the traditional sense, but you are a player, and the role you play might be called "outsider." But it is still a role in the political drama.

- *Consider the political side.* As you accomplish your goals, get the political support you need to succeed. Take action that is good for the organization while holding to your values.

- *Know what you want.* Chapter 3 talked about YOU and WANTS: "Pursuing Your Aspirations." Give a lot of attention to your

WANTS. Revisit them daily. Notice how you are living by what you want and value. Practice defining and expressing what you want. Say it aloud to others. Make sure this is what you believe.

- *Know what you will and will not do in politics.* Decide how you will participate. Think this out ahead of your actions. Be able to express actions you are willing and unwilling to take. Find your limits.

Building a Positive Political Climate

You are helping establish the political climate of your organization. Whether you are trying to figure out how to help the investment club president decide it is time to step down, or you are withholding your thoughts during a meeting or when confronting a senior official, you are one of many people defining the politics here. Since there is no rule book, understand that rules are being written over and over again in the minds of the people playing. New rules are tried, and they succeed or fail. This is where you have a chance to influence the climate. No, you will not change it to your liking overnight, but your day-to-day actions will affect it. And even when that effect seems negligible, you will know. If your bias is toward more open and fair politics, some of these ideas could be useful:

- *Deal with people face-to-face.* Politics is based on established relationships of loyalty and trust. Relationships are established best through one-to-one meetings of the key invested people, not through e-mails, phone calls, or faxes. Find constructive ways to meet with the people you wish to influence.

- *Find shared WANTS.* Shared wants give others a reason to meet with you, so discover what it is that you want together and need to talk about. This straightforward approach, when it works, undermines unspoken, behind-the-scenes negotiations.

- *Take the larger, longer view.* This is usually the more generous and open stance. It counters those who are more focused on immediate and narrow outcomes. Take the position that is open to other points of view.

- *Use openness to counter secrets.* Politics often has to do with who talks to whom about what. Negative politics often puts tight limits on sharing of information. Develop a bias toward sharing information widely.

- *Increase your tolerance of ambiguity.* Loaded political situations often push combatants to immovable, polar positions. Learn to hold your opinions in abeyance while you sincerely explore alternatives offered by others.

- *Be willing to understand others.* This is essential to dialogue and breaks down political barriers. By doing this, you encourage others to do the same.

- *Remind yourself that understanding does not mean agreement.* It is possible for you to listen to me, understand what I say, and hold a different point of view. In fact, when people of differing views try to get something done together, it is essential for them to hear each other in order to discover what they can do together. Negative politics often builds distances between disagreeing people, reducing the likelihood of common understanding. Set up opportunities where disagreeing parties can recognize their shared goals, understand each other, clarify their disagreements, and explore alternative actions that they all can support. Disagreement does not preclude collaborative action.

Working Through Negative Political Situations

Success in politically charged situations is enhanced when, from the beginning, you are thinking about the ending you want. Without the guidance of your wants for yourself and others, you will likely get lost along the way. And you may stray into behavior that is inconsistent with what you really want—if you had only taken time to figure that out first. The path through a political minefield could be charted with these steps:

1. **OUTCOMES**: Remind yourself of the outcomes you want to achieve. Outcomes include what others will know at the end of your work together, what they will do, and how they will feel as a result of your work. Outcomes also relate to you: How will you feel, what will you do, what will you know as a result of this encounter? This is a critical step.

2. OPTIONS: Survey all of your options: What could you do or say that would make it more likely you could achieve the outcomes you want? Be open in your search for options while withholding judgment.

3. WANT: Of the options, which do you want to do? Which do you not want to do? Which are you open or not open to doing? This step allows you to consider your politics in relation to others' politics. This is where your values meaningfully limit the options you will consider. All the while, keep in mind the outcomes you want for yourself and others.

4. CHOICE: Decide which path will most likely lead you to the desired results within the values you hold.

5. ACT: Act, and explain the reasons for your actions to others, including the political considerations.

These five steps do not necessarily happen sequentially. More likely, you will jump around the process as you adapt to the reality facing you. But try to keep the outcomes that you desire foremost in your mind—especially those that relate to values and feelings. When others leave an encounter feeling good about it, they will be more likely to return to talk again.

Return to your earlier thoughts and feelings about politics. Perhaps, by putting my experiences and ideas beside your own, new options are opened for you. Politics are not easy to understand, to change, or to avoid. There is a political reality in every organization, even those that espouse their freedom from politics. Face the reality and learn from it if you want to get things done.

CHAPTER EIGHT

Seek the Priorities

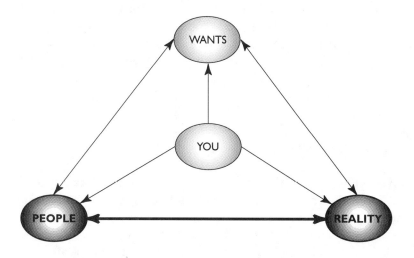

The theme of an earlier chapter was "Build Common Understanding." This chapter's theme of "Seek the Priorities" could be seen as a corollary. Organizations are put together to move us in a common, clear, shared direction, though they seldom work that way. The accelerating pace of change in the world around us shifts priorities constantly—often even before the ink has set on the spreadsheet coming out of the printer. We increasingly live in a world of quick response based more on informed intuition than printed plans. The priorities of the moment become more important than the printed plan. Yes, the priorities usually bow in the direction of the plan, but they have much more life in them.

When managers and decision makers cannot plan fast enough to keep up, they need to rely more on the expertise of people like you. This absence of plans is not the disaster some people talk about. For you—it's an opportunity! In fact, it just may be that *knowing* the priorities of the organizations is worse than not knowing, especially if you want to shape those priorities. When the organization is not loudly and widely declaring what is important, you have more room to decide for yourself. Perhaps no position has been taken and you can take it. Successful change makers often capitalize on the organization that has yet to declare its direction.

If the organization does have priorities at this moment, how do you find them? How do you influence them? Better yet, how do you *set* them? The answers to these three questions shift as much as the ground that organizations are built upon, but the following points lead you in the right direction. Keep in mind that each of these points can move you to better understand the reality of the organization as it is now; changing it is another matter and the subject of other chapters. In the rest of this chapter, we will consider money, time, and your power as indicators of priority.

Follow the Money

Money is one of the primary indicators of what this organization values. For-profit or not-for-profit, rich organization or poor organization—where the money goes sends major messages to all involved. You don't have to like this reality, but ignore it at your peril! Follow the money and it will almost always lead you to where the organization is placing its priorities right now. This may or may not fit with what it says is important. If you are part of an organization that has a budget, see where it goes. Money is seldom evenly distributed; even distribution would say that everything is equally important. Not true. There are reasons behind where the money goes; find out what they are. Find out in a way that is more objective than envious, more analytical than jealous. Worry less about the justice or injustice of your share and learn more about how and why people got what they got. Budgets and financial plans are increasingly available across organizations. There is much you can learn from them, perhaps through seeking the help of others who know more about them.

Trace the Time

Just as money is an indicator of present priorities, so is time. What is this organization spending time on? How much time is being given to what processes, content, and actions? Where do the decision makers routinely invest their time? The answers to these questions indicate what is important—not necessarily what *should be* important, but what *is* important. If you are not getting time from decision makers, you are at a disadvantage relative to those who are getting time.

Getting things done requires face-to-face time with decision makers. And this does not mean rushing a memo by the executive director for his signature, or a 10-minute board presentation that no one comments on, or a committee's quick approval of a new process. No, it means discussing important issues *at length* with key people. It means building relationships that allow you to drop by informally to test an idea. It means being able to argue a point on equal footing with a decision maker so that you each know you have been heard.

This must be quality time; quantity time is not enough. Without quality, you will not continue to get on the decision makers' calendar. Pay attention to *their* definition of quality if you want to see them again. Those who succeed get time with key decision makers because that is where ideas are moved into action. Those key people only have so much calendar time available; they will try to fill that space with their most important work. Each calendar entry reduces the time available. One meeting crowded in means something else is crowded out. We have all been crowded in and crowded out. What are the patterns in your organization? What and who continually succeeds in getting time with decision makers? What do they do that works?

There is not enough time to do everything that is important. Life and work continually ask us to choose a few from the many priorities before us. When we hear ourselves saying "It's important to me, but not right now," we are saying that this is not important enough for me to give time to, or act upon—meaning it is not really important. Notice this in yourself; notice it in your organization. What gets lip service but not calendar time? Accepting this reality is a step toward doing something to elevate it in importance or downgrade it and drop it.

A little on-the-ground research into the realities of how this organization works can serve you in many ways: You will better understand the larger organizational realities, stepping beyond your smaller piece to see it all. In effect, you are taking on a higher leadership perspective. You will learn how others manage to get money for projects and time with decision makers, how they succeed and fail. You will borrow their ideas, and perhaps give them a few of your own. Your new relationships with others will be useful in future work with them.

Find Your Power

Consider the conversations that come down to "They have power . . .
We don't . . . They won't change . . . We can do nothing!" If you were to
believe that, what power would you have? How would you feel about
your role, your effectiveness, yourself? Imagine the framework, the assumptions, and the behaviors that come with this way of thinking and
feeling. Imagine the effort required to show up for work, "knowing"
how hopeless the situation is. People feeling this way about their work
must have very compelling reasons for continuing. Power and power-
lessness begin in our personal needs and assumptions, and then play
out in our actions. The power we have and that we assign to others is
largely a matter of perception. Right now, a power exchange of sorts is
taking place between us. You, the reader, are giving some power to me;
you know more about that than I do. And I, the writer, am giving some
power to you; my assumptions about you show in the way that I write.
Power is part of any important dynamic between people.

Formal power, authority, gets an inordinate amount of attention
in most organizations. A few people have it and most of us don't; that's
the way most of our hierarchical organizations are built. Absence of
formal power can result in our longing for it and accentuating its importance. "There are so many things I could do if only I had power." For
some of us, expressing this notion gives us the excuse we need to not
act. It is as if recognizing our self-defined sorry state absolves us from
doing anything about it. How much of our energy do we spend envying
powers that others have? How much time do we waste decrying what
we lack? How often do we give up, saying that we can't do anything because we don't have any power? Decrying what we lack and someone
else possesses does not build our power.

In our power fantasies, many of us imagine much about the
power that others have, especially "management." Back in reality,
their powers are usually different from, and smaller than, we imagine. Most of the power management has exists because we give it to
them; we see them as powerful. Other people do the same with us.
People give or take away our power based on the type and amount of
power they think we have. As mentioned earlier, much power is in
perception, both self-perception and others' perceptions. When you
think you are powerful, you *are* more powerful. Believing in your
ability to get what you want will move you to actions that a less-
believing-you would not consider. When others think you are powerful, you *are*. When they believe in your ability to get what you want,

they give you power. Power has deeper sources than belief, but belief helps.

Whether leading your life or leading a committee meeting, you have powers at your disposal. Whether you think of yourself as a powerful person or not, powers come with your various roles in work and life. When you accept your roles in organizations as given, you look to the organization to tell you what to do and are biased toward accepting that guidance. In that case, you would see your formal role as rather static, rather than as a starting point. As an actor in each of your accepted roles, you shape the role as you perform it. Where do you look for guidance in shaping your role? The organization? Yourself? Others? Your answers build from your assumptions.

AN EXERCISE

Building Formal Power

The formal power you have may be small, but you need to understand it as a legitimate power coming from outside yourself. You are not limited to your formal authority, but it provides a base to build upon. Follow these steps to discover what your role is, what you want it to be, and what it can be.

1. *Find out what your role is.* What is written about it, said about it, and universally agreed upon? Collect this information and understand it as you begin.

2. *Find out how it is working.* Talk with people who deal with you in the role. Do they understand how to work with you? Who uses you in the role particularly well? Who regularly has problems?

3. *Describe the authority you want in order to carry out your role.* What decisions would you like to make? How would you like to involve others?

4. *Compare the authority you have and what you want,* the want and the reality. What is working? What is not? What actions would you like to take?

5. *Test.* Who else needs to know about what you have discovered and what you want? Whose support do you need? Who might be threatened by the changes you would like to make? Engage them and get their support.

6. *Act.* Try some of your new actions, a few at a time, with sensitivity toward others.

7. *Check.* When you shift your role, how is it working for you? For others? Note the differences.

Formal authority is part of the reality of our organizational lives. Organizationally backed authority is just one useful way of getting what you want; it is not the only way and usually not the best way—even for those people who have it. As a governor told me once: "Yes, I could tell them to do it; I have that power. But I can use up that power very quickly and end up with a bunch of people doing only what I want to do. That's not good enough. Whatever they do, I want them to choose to do it." He was aware of the limits to his formal power; he knew the better path was often withholding demands and trying to enlist people's support. Those of us without the formal authority might fantasize about how we would use it if we had it, but how do those fantasies match what works in the real world?

When working with someone who has authority, do not deal with that authority as *the* compelling reality; instead, see their authority as one useful tool among many. Do not ignore their authority; that will not help your work relationship with them. See their authority as another resource available to you—much as they might see your expertise as a resource available to them.

CHAPTER NINE

Who Makes a Difference?

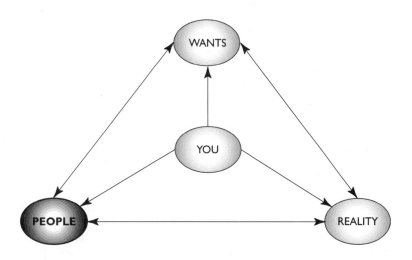

The organization world is giving increasing emphasis to the importance of PEOPLE. This is not news, but its truth is being underlined in this information age when the unique talents of human beings are more important to work than ever before. Organizations need human hearts and minds, not just muscle. Whether working on new software or a child education project, PEOPLE must invest deeply to assure success. The challenge seems to be shared everywhere: How do we get the right PEOPLE to invest in this organization? (For example, the construction company that is offering employees bonuses and vacations for attracting new employees, or the environmental foundation that is figuring out how to build a board of directors that will attract and retain talented people.)

Accomplishment depends on the PEOPLE in this corner of the GTD model, and the question is "Who makes a difference?" Who affects, or is affected by, the move from REALITY toward WANTS. These are the PEOPLE who must take responsibility for REALITY, aspire to the WANTS, and take action. YOU must work with and through these PEOPLE if you are to get anything done. Without those PEOPLE, YOU become the third corner of the model, and it is all up to YOU. Life has probably already taught you that this does not work. Consider the many people you interact with in your work, community, and personal life:

Parents	Peers
Customers	Spouse
Work group	Volunteers
Consultants	Customers
Board members	Management
Citizens	Boss
Friends	Children
Suppliers	Listserve
Therapist	Coach

Add your people to mine and you get some sense of the variety of people who might help or hinder you. Depending on what is happening, combinations of these people can emerge as important to what you are trying to accomplish. A current project may involve only a few of them; a holiday party might involve them all.

Imagine that all the important people in your life are gathered in front of you, that you are on a raised platform from which you can see all of them. If you like give yourself a scepter, a crown, and a throne. Now imagine that each person present tells you, and all those assembled, the support they could put at your disposal. Imagine the time, talent, counsel, money, authority, information, affection, equipment, networking, enthusiasm, power, loyalty, perseverance, vision, and values they could bring to you. Imagine that, while you are listening, someone is charting all these wonderful resources on a huge wall chart—perhaps a matrix with people's names down one side and resources across the top—and checking in the boxes where there is a match. What an impressive chart that would be! To go a step further, imagine the hundreds of other PEOPLE that are connected to the PEOPLE on the chart, and how their resources might be available to YOU.

Leave the fantasy and bring the wall chart with you, because in one sense it is real. All those people with all those resources are out there right now; you have only to call on them. Though this can be as simple as asking, that is not usually the case. For YOU, at the center of the GTD model, each person represents an opportunity. Perhaps what you WANT fits with what they WANT, moving them in your direction. This might be an opportunity for them. All of these people represent resources. YOU have to discover the resources PEOPLE have, and then decide whether and how to enlist those resources—without the benefit of a scepter or crown. And, you can do this through an open process that respects the PEOPLE and what they bring.

AN EXERCISE

Successful Work Relationships

Take five minutes to work through these five steps:

1. Think of one work relationship that lasted at least a few months and was especially successful and rewarding to you. It may have been paid or volunteer work, recent or distant past; the only requirements are that it involved other people, you found it rewarding, and it lasted a while.

2. Note five words or phrases that describe why this relationship was so rewarding. Putting them on paper will work better than holding them in your head.

3. Add your phrases to these I have collected from others:

Accomplishment	Did a good job
Enjoyable	Great outcome
Hard work together	Learned a lot
Mutual respect	Done on time
Fun	Caring
Trust	Defied the odds
The risk involved	Recognition
Satisfaction	High point in my work

4. Note the phrases that fit with your rewarding relationship.

5. Notice how many of your selections could fit with a description of friendship. Mark all those that do.

For many people, this exercise makes the often-unspoken point: We work for reasons beyond the recognition we receive in praise or pay, or the contribution we make; we seek human contact, caring, and love through our work. For some of us, that is just a bonus added to the satisfaction of the work itself; for others, the work is the bonus added to the friendships built through that work. Regardless of where you may find yourself on this matter, it has great importance to this PEOPLE corner of the triangle.

If many people do seek caring and friendship through their work, this suggests a lot about how you might approach the PEOPLE in your life. You might start with the assumption that this is potentially more than just a work relationship; there is the possibility of friendship at some level. Just carrying that assumption to work would affect your behavior. And you would likely act noticeably different from a person focused on work and work alone. All of your interactions would be influenced by these larger-than-work possibilities.

All of these PEOPLE possess resources, but they are more than just resources. They must be dealt with as people if they are to offer what they have to you. This means respecting who they are and what they offer. The ideas that follow can aid you in dealing with people— and aid them in dealing with each other.*

Help Those Whom You Would Have Help You

Yes, the proverbial wisdom of the Golden Rule—and do we ever need it! Most people are not required to lend you their resources, so you must search for what would allow them to want to help you. Take your mind off yourself and put it on them; ask how you can help them get what they want. Look at it this way: Do you want them to help *you* get what *you* want? Yes? Then help *them* get what *they* want. Go out of your way to discover what they want and help them get it. See Chapter 12 for

---

*See my book, *The Beauty of the Beast: Breathing New Life into Organizations*, for elaboration on related points.

more on this. You enhance the likelihood of your own success by helping other reach for theirs.

Respect the Past

There were people with ability and ideas in this organization before you came along. In fact, you are now building on the base established before you got here. Learn from their past and the organization's past. Leaps into the future seldom succeed by separating from what has gone before. Use your opportunities to praise what others have done to help the organization move to this point in its history. Be especially attentive to recent contributions made by people who are still here and likely to be important to its future. Knowing the history of a place allows you to honor it—and others to appreciate you for recognizing it.

Deal Openly

There is a high potential for manipulation when you are dealing with other people because you want something from them. I have heard myself secretly saying "I know what I want...now...how do I get them to think it's their idea?" Following this secret path too frequently damages the very relationships you need to build. Be open and realistic with others. Tell them you need their help. Ask how you can help them. Be candid about what you are doing with them, why you are doing it, how you expect this will serve you, and how it will serve them. They often will match your openness with their own.

Manipulators withhold information from others to increase power over them. It is manipulative to use tactics on a person and not acknowledge what you are doing. And it is manipulative to exaggerate a point, or to lie, so that the other person will see reality differently. I have done this, but I am not proud of it. These are not the behaviors for us to aspire to, if we want to build longstanding relationships with others. In the long run, manipulation does not give us what we want.

Create Your Relationship Web

Picture yourself as a spider at the center of a large web made up of those people most important in your life. You spun the web, connecting you to all the important corners of your life. It is your web; you are at its center, and you maintain it religiously. When something hits your web, you run out to discover what it is, to store it or ingest it. If the web needs repair, you do it, and then you return to its center, waiting for something else to happen. This is sounding a bit predatory, but I still like the web-building and tending parts of the image.

We can use the spider's web to consider our relationship web. Our web is as vital for our success as it is for a spider's. Our web, or network, feeds us with the information we need to tell what is going on. Each of us must spin our own web and maintain it. The web provides us with both information and access to the people of influence and power. But, different from the spiders, our web joins with the webs of other key people, becoming three-dimensional. We spin webs that extend out to people, all those PEOPLE we discussed earlier, engaging their knowledge, skill, authority, power, influence, caring, and energy.

Web maintenance is a key to getting things done. Like the spider, if we do not keep our web of relationships in shape, it will not be there when we need it. This takes time, and lots of it—a real issue in today's accelerated work world. You may recall the last time you found that your web was tattered and torn (like when you are on your way to meet with someone to ask a favor, someone you have not seen in a long time. . . and the last time you saw her was to ask for a favor). We must maintain and reweave the web, for it to feed us. Maintenance means regular contact with the people it is connected to—and not just when we need their help. Instead, we should be out there ahead of time, updating them on what is going on and offering to help them with their priorities. Continued work on the web ensures that, when we need assistance, we are well connected to the people who can help.

Identify the people with whom you need formal and informal contact. List them and get others' help with this list. Assess your present relationship with each of these individuals and compare it to what you would like it to be. Decide on some specific actions you could take to build relationships. Establish the web by paying sincere attention to others. Listen to what they have to say. Help them get things done. Cultivate relationships with people *before* you want something of them, fully knowing that you may never ask them for anything. This makes it more likely that they will have time for you when you need time.

Web-spinning is a long term process. You do it for what you, others, and the organization might want tomorrow, not for something you needed yesterday.

The web is particularly important for those of us working with lots of heart but little authority. Established relationships assure us of getting the information we need about important matters in the organization and also establish the privilege of being able to influence key decision makers who are part of our web. With our web in place, we know where to go to gather or present information. We have an essential, if wispy, network for influencing organization directions. Without it, we are much less powerful.

CHAPTER TEN

Enlist Able Partners

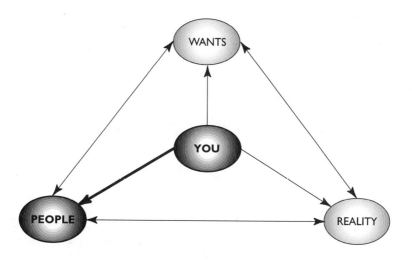

Partner with **PEOPLE** to achieve what **YOU** and they **WANT**. Enlist their commitment and resources, and your job will be made easier—especially over the long term. Much of what you know about the other elements of the GTD model is applied in the dynamic between **YOU** and the key **PEOPLE** around you. This is where work relationships are formed. Whether you are "in charge" or not, think *partnership* if you want to succeed in today's organizations. When you have some authority, use it as *a* source of power, but not *the only* source of power. Focusing only on your authority will reduce your options for constructive action with others—especially given the fact that you don't have authority over that many people in this world. Solid sense tells you that knowing how to work with others as partners is necessary to your success. This chapter offers many ways of doing that.*

---

*Adapted from my chapter in *Moving from Training to Performance,* by Dana G. Robinson and James C. Robinson, eds., Berrett-Koehler and ASTD, co-publishers, 1998.

The larger the organization, the more partnership required. Picture partnership as people linked by clasped hands. Now, picture a large and effective organization held together by hundreds of partnerships. . . hundreds, thousands of people clasping hands. . . linking, depending on each other. That image is a better representation of what goes on in our organizations than the boxy charts we so often use to show how the place works. Much of what we will discuss here applies beyond work relationships to social partnerships, friendships, and even marriage. We can learn from all forms of partnership as we consider how to build the working relationships we want with key people around us.

The Parts in Partnership

A partner is a person who "takes part" with others. So partnership has to do with "parts", as in, "What parts do we play in this work we do together?" That question contains the three primary elements of partnership: Purpose, Roles, and Partnering. Partnering is the result of pursuing Purpose and Roles.

- **Purpose:** This is what brings us together in the first place. Our continuing contact in a work setting is justified by service to a larger purpose. No purpose? No partnership. It may be buried in a flurry of busy-ness that never asks the question "Why are we doing this?" Foggy, clear, implicit, or explicit purpose is always there.

- **Role:** We are particularly interested in your role as you work with others. Your role emphasizes personal clarity and competence combined with adaptability as you focus on what your partner brings and wants. This includes your clarity about your purposes, your knowledge of your competence and potential contribution, your awareness of the needs of your partner, your interpersonal skills, your ability to develop alternatives and bring new perspective, and your willingness to risk. You cannot control, or count on, what the potential partner will bring, but you can control what *you* bring.

- **Partnering:** When you and another decide to pursue purpose together, partnering is the visible and invisible dynamic between you and the other person(s). Partnering is usually focused on the work at hand, but it is much larger than that. Partnering taps into underlying assumptions, trust and risk, shared values, and expectations. Often these key elements are unexpressed, many are irrational, and all require attention to succeed in the work at hand. If you attend to roles and purposes but neglect building the partnership, you set yourselves up to fail in your work together.

Anticipating Success

We form partnerships in anticipation of success. We, the partners, define the success we seek. Questions like these help partners anticipate, not just the traditional outcome of the project, but what happens along the way: "If we were successful doing this together, what would our results look like?" "What would have to happen for you to call this effort a success?" "How will you know if this work is succeeding?" "What do you think is working about what we are doing right now?" "How is this meeting/report giving you what you want?" These questions pursue accomplishment and achievement, rather than caution and avoidance of failure. The tone resulting from the discussion supports good work together.

Contracts and Contracting

Everyone working with, playing with, and living with other people is behaving within implicit contracts. Each of us pays attention to how we relate to, perform with, and interact with the people around us. Even when standing silently on an elevator, a deal is in the making, about how close we will stand to each other and whether we will talk. Here we will talk about contracts between you and key people but, as the example illustrates, contracting is going on everywhere. Where there are work partnerships, there are contracts.

A contract is "the deal" within which people play out their relationship. It is about what we each are willing to give and what we want in return. Some form of contract is always there, whether discussed or not, whether mutually understood or not—and that contract becomes the basis for building solid partnerships. We need to understand the importance of contracting; we need to help our partners be more explicit about what they want and what they offer.

A distinction can be made between "the contract" and *contracting*. *A contract is the present mutual understanding of who will do what to achieve purpose.* Notice the aliveness of that statement:

- "The present . . . understanding" (not yesterday's or tomorrow's, but today's)

- " . . . mutual understanding . . ." (not what the partners might understand separately)

- " . . . who will do what . . . " (this is the part of a contract with which we are most familiar)

- " . . . to achieve purpose." (this reminds us that the partners are together because something larger is being served)

You often think of your work with others in terms of your current projects and programs. That is important, but contracts and contracting are larger than these immediate considerations. You probably care about building long-term relationships with key people; about forging a continuiing partnership. These two needs suggest two levels of contracting: an explicit level, in which you and others actively engage in contracting to do current work this week or this month, and an implicit level, in which you and others are engaged in building and maintaining a work relationship that lasts years, rather than months or days. The difference between these two levels is like the difference between a date and marriage. The explicit contract carries a sense of immediacy; there is no commitment beyond the task at hand. Of course, there is the possibility of something more beyond this "date," but that is not part of the deal. The implicit contract grows through time on the strength of the explicit work done and contracts completed. Eventually the two parties recognize the potential for a long-term partnership. And, if they talk with each other about this work relationship, they are likely discussing the opportunities inherent in committing more deeply to each other for the long term. As you can imagine—or have experienced—this is quite a different discussion from signing up for just another work project.

Solid partnerships grow from clear contracting, with emphasis on the contract**ing**. It is the dynamic of contracting on which partnerships thrive. Explicit agreements between partners to keep each other informed allow their living contracts to change. The shifting world requires the partners adapt to a new reality, a reality that wasn't present or forecast when they began work together. Their commitment to contracting anticipates unknown changes. To keep partnerships alive through contracting, talk about the working relationship between you. For example, talk about how well your initial meeting with each other went and the roles that each of you are taking on. Notice your partner's receptiveness to this and adjust accordingly. Do not be surprised if she has not stepped back from your work together to notice how you are doing it. You both can be so focused on the immediate task that you miss the opportunity to think about effective ways of building your partnership.

Ask your potential partners about successful work partnerships they have had in the past. Share a few experiences of your own. Then ask them what they expect from this partnership with you. Write this down so you can use it in the future. The first time you and a partner agree on the nature of the work and your roles, write it down—not because this is a legal contract, but because you will forget. Build in regular meetings with them to talk about how the work is going and how your partnership contributes to or detracts from that. Check regularly and informally with them on how the work is going and always be ready to tell them how it is going for you. Occasionally, do this more formally. Write it down, put it before them, and take time to talk about it. Look for other ways to make contracting a natural part of the work you do with others. Connect your discussions of the partnership to "real work." Connect the success you are having to the success of your partnership.

When the partnership is not working, when the contract is being twisted, when you have nagging doubts about what is happening, bring it up. Use the contract you have between you as the way of bringing it up. For example: "I was just looking back on the agreements we made as we began this process. I'd like for us to talk about them again. What do you think?" or "When do you think we could sit down and take a look at our work? Let's get it on our calendars." Continual contracting keeps the partnership vital and successful. Do not treat the contract and the contracting process legalistically—that will choke the life out of it. Keep the contract alive by regularly revisiting it and never finishing it.

Partnership agreements extend to more than just a few people. Think about a project you have coming up, or one you have worked on recently. List each of the key people and groups important to this project. As you build the list, notice how different they are, and how different their expectations are. Positive results usually means dealing with the whole array of expectations generated by the project. It's a challenge to build an array of key partnerships, each tailored to the purposes and needs of a particular person and yourself. Seeing your array of partnerships gives you a glimpse into why organizations with hundreds or thousands of people and partnerships are so difficult to change.

Your Unique Value-Added Contribution

Partnership has more to do with "doing your part" than equality. Its emphasis is less on whether partners have equal power and more on whether each contributes uniquely to results. Too often I have seen myself or others striving for equal power, giving too much attention to hierarchy and stature. That misses the point. The basis for partnership is in the answer to this question: What is your unique, value-added contribution? When you and your potential partners agree on your answers to this question, you have each identified the ingredients you bring to create a little magic together—because that is just how partnership can feel!

I have noticed that many people choose to work with me because I am similar to them in some significant ways. Perhaps we have a related work background, or read similar books, or share an interest in technology. That is what gets us started, but often they continue working with me because I am different from them. *After we build the relationship and mutual trust based on our similarities, we can capitalize on our differences.* Romantic relationships and friendships often show the same pattern: During early acquaintance, couples or new friends often remark on how similar they are, how they experience the world in the same way. Years later, their relationship will likely be enriched by the differences between them. As Sheila Kelly, my partner for over 40 years, says, "The reasons we got married and the reasons we stay married are different." And so it is with the "marriages" in the workplace. Check this observation with your experience.

Similarities between partners at work contribute to the comfort and predictability of the relationship—and we certainly need a dose of that. The dissimilarities are the source of creativity and friction, opportunity and risk—we need this too. It takes all the awareness we can muster to stay on top of these conflicting expectations and continue to be a well-aligned professional. When we are most effective as partners, we help others understand our uniqueness and how it might be applied to the work at hand. Focusing on our unique, value-added contribution turns us toward the intrapersonal and intraprofessional. When others choose to work with you, what do they get that is special? What do you reliably and repeatedly bring to work that others value? Over the years, what have you heard from partners about your positive contributions? The answers to these questions are about your unique, value-added contribution.

Partnership Begins with You

A first step in building partnerships is to be—and be seen as—someone with whom others want to partner. Succeed on the organization's terms as well as your own, and do it in a way that others can see your success. Many relationships lack the potential for true partnership because one of the parties lacks the grounding in success for which the other partners are looking. Or, someone who aspires to be a partner has a strong record of success but potential partners don't know about it. Success will be defined differently in the Port Authority, the PTA, and the Young President's Association, but it is valued and honored in all organizations.

If you want to partner with others, then be seen as successful. Do whatever you want others to do for themselves. Model the very behaviors that you would like to see in your partners. If you think partnership involves speaking openly about concerns, do that with them. If you think partnership includes regular meetings, propose that. In all the work you do, pay attention to the kind of partner that you are and that they are. All of this makes you a more attractive partner, and others around you at work are likely to notice. The next time they need a good partner, they are more likely to look your way. Think of the options this could open for you.

Build a Pattern of Accomplishments

Some of us wish and wait for the "big score"—the one project or program that calls out all of our skills and garners all the recognition we could ever hope for. We judge work in terms of its potential impact and visibility: Little impact and visibility means it's of little interest to us. On the other hand, some of us seek the smaller projects that are important to a few people and not all that visible in the organization. No awards, no articles in the newsletter, just a small, solid contribution. When we do this, we build a pattern of small accomplishments and a small, solid reputation for success. And, each project under our belt adds to our expertise and earns some trust and respect.

The last few sentences are the working strategy for many successful

-and-not-in-charge people. It is not the "right" strategy, but it is an alternative that more of us could use. There are risks in using it: You risk being buried in trivial pursuits, you endanger your longer-range perspective, you give yourself over to other people's priorities, and you may lose sight of your functional priorities. But it can work when pursued very intentionally with the idea of building your pattern of accomplishment and building a reputation for success in your organization. And, of course, you will learn a lot along the way.

Pass the Word on Your Success

You need recognition for success to be seen as an attractive partner. Help others learn about what you have done. Don't expect them to find out; they are too busy with their own work and lives to seek out your accomplishments. Nobody is going to ask you to dance if you are hiding in a corner. Get out in the light where they can see you. No, this does not mean constantly pointing to yourself and showing off. For good reasons, most of us shrink from that kind of self-promotion. What you need to do is much more subtle than that. It can be telling someone that you want to review your work with them, to get their ideas. Or, it might be asking someone to sit down with you and help you plan the coming year. Or, you might convene a small group to discuss an organizational issue, where in the process everyone talks about their experience dealing with related issues. Or, it might be e-mailing a paper around, asking for comments.

There are four ingredients in each of the above examples: (1) your accomplishment and talents get discussed, (2) in a setting that allows wider consideration of what you might do, (3) by others who see a link between your work and their interests, and (4) they get to contribute to you while learning about you. This is different from standing up in a meeting and bragging about yourself to a group of people who have not declared their interest. The next point is a corollary to spreading the word on your success.

Expect Less Appreciation

Have you ever noticed that when you do good work the recipients are not as grateful as they ought to be? Have you ever spent weeks on a project and not even gotten a thank you? Have you ever wanted to scream at someone who dismisses your work by giving it far less time than it deserves? If any of this troubles you, try this counter-intuitive perspective: Of course they don't appreciate what you've done. Of course they don't thank you. Of course they don't give you time. If you were in their position, you probably wouldn't either. In fact, there's a good chance that someone else has similar complaints about you. If you cannot find someone at work who feels under-appreciated by you, go home and ask there!

Most organizations encourage people to look anxiously to the future while assuming the past is not worth talking about—unless there is a problem. The work you do is part of something larger; it is not appreciated but expected: *What have you done for me lately?* No, this is not wonderful or right, but it is understandable. Appreciation gets crowded out in our hectic reach for tomorrow; the formal and informal structures we build have a hard time accommodating something as squishy as appreciation. When organizations specialize, people's duties and responsibilities are narrowed. In focusing on the big picture, the little people get blurred. The larger the organization, the more true this is likely to be, but even members of small volunteer organizations suffer from working alone, investing their all, and no one knowing it. It does not need to be this way, and you can do something to change it. Appreciate someone each day, in honest and specific terms. Watch them light up. And, when you do not get the appreciation you deserve, search for the reasons while accepting the reality.

Accept Others' Lack of Knowledge

An association of twenty city neighborhoods asked a meeting consultant to design and run their quarterly meeting. They asked for help because their meetings frequently yielded more frustration than results. The consultant did as she was asked and did it well. She kept the group focused on the agenda, achieved balanced participation, sought and clarified decisions. The participants got the results they wanted, congratulated themselves, gave the exhausted consultant some polite thank you's, and left. The consultant was disappointed and angry and called me to unload. After all the work she did before and during the meeting! What an ungrateful bunch! She was finished with this work and not interested in more.

But their behavior does make some ironic sense. The neighborhood association called because their meetings were not working. Said differently, they did not know how to run a good meeting. Since they did not know how, they might not know why a meeting is working when it does work. They do not have the eye or the lens through which to appreciate what happened. They liked the results, but could not recognize the subtle methods used to help them get those results. The consultant expected them to deeply appreciate what she had done *and* it was lack of that ability that caused them to call in the first place!

You may have seen a version of this story in the groups with which you work. Much of the understanding, gratitude, and appreciation we are expecting is unreasonable, considering others' knowledge of our work and our needs. Yes, they could better appreciate what we put before them—even when they do not know what went into it. But we might as well let go of our expectation that they will wax eloquent on the subtleties of our contribution. This dream might only be realized if people who have a deep understanding of our work are there when we do it. When you are in deep need of affirmation, bring along a co-worker who knows and can appreciate what you do.

Ask About What They Care About

When you want people to see you as a potential partner, ask them questions that draw on their expertise. Others move closer to you when you ask about *them* rather than tell about you. People are experts on what they do and how they do it, and many of them like to talk about it. As a result of your insightful questions and interest, they will probably think you are interesting and smart. Ask them what they do and listen to the answers. Or, ask what they like about this work. Or, ask what is getting in the way of their doing the work. Or, what helps them do their work. Do not start off by telling about yourself or asking how they might work with you. Instead focus on what they know and care about. Follow their answers to find the path to partnership between you. And in all of this, show your respect for what they do. We all want to be respected.

Risk Seeing It Their Way

Another application of the Golden Rule: Listen to others as you would have them listen to you. Take off your defensive battle gear and listen for the content and feelings of that person with whom you have so much difficulty. Risk understanding his message. Risk confusion as you put his thoughts next to your own. Risk converting to his view as you understand it better. After all, isn't that what you expect of him? You limit the possibilities for partnership when you avoid an encounter with that person, or when you are determined to leave holding the same views you came in with.

Say Yes . . .
and Say No

Look for opportunities to say yes. The exciting work in your future will come from what you say yes to. Some of us are overworked and reactively say no as we protect ourselves. But, for our lives to continue to be interesting, we have to say yes to something new occasionally. In saying yes, we can be guided by what we want; we need to remind ourselves of that. We can be guided by what our organization wants. Seek partnerships that involve saying yes to something you and your partners want to do together. Saying yes to high-priority projects can mean dropping other work in which you are already involved. So be it. Saying yes to some things and not to others defines what is important to you and helps you get what you want.

When you have to say no, say it clearly and politely. Even say it less politely, but *do* say it! Many of us hesitate to say that we will not do what is being asked of us. Who knows what causes this reluctance: the desire to be liked, the notion we can do it all, not wanting to miss out on anything. Partnerships build better on truth and reliability than on misinformation and distortion. Do not lead partners into believing that you are planning to act when you are not. They would much rather know that you are not going to act than be fooled into thinking you are. Sure, they might leave the conversation upset because you won't give them what they want. They may understand why you said no, or they may not. But, in the long run, your reputation for truth and reliability will win out over their immediate disappointment.

If you work in a group of interdependent people and say no as a pattern, you may build a naysaying reputation. People—especially partners—will grow weary of continual no's. The result is, some good ideas may stop before they even get to you. Saying no is one of the ways you define your personal boundaries; saying yes is the other part. Together they declare what you stand for and will act upon. They help others know what to expect from you.

Long-Term Partnerships

One real indicator of your success is repeat business. When people choose to work with you again and again, you know they see value in your work. These long-term relationships are the ones that most of us like to cultivate—and that many of us must cultivate—to insure we have a job. We can make it more likely that these partnerships develop by attending to what we want and discussing this with others key to the work. Support those discussions with strong patterns of accomplishment and you are on your way to building the long-term relationship you desire. Part of your challenge is to help others see the value of what you have been doing. The people we work with will be inclined to focus on what is most important to them, preventing them from seeing what we have accomplished for them. Give them the data they need to recognize your patterns of accomplishment in your working partnership with them. This lays the groundwork for a long-term partnership.

If you want to build long-term partnerships, ask yourself: Is there a pattern of accomplishment in the work you have done with them? Practical people want to invest in partners who have demonstrated a repeated ability to succeed. Build that pattern and help your partners see it. Your sequential success with them will build their confidence in you. Consider: Do you respect your partners? Do you respect what they do? Their intentions? Their aspirations? Their characters? If you do, show it. If you do not, you will not be able to hide this over the long term and you will be caught in your charade. Find other partners or other work.

In most of my older work partnerships, I am valued not just as an expert or a hard worker but as an individual. Those partnerships have grown into personal relationships. I don't know any other way to grow a partnership that lasts for many years without making it personal. You may know how, but I don't. What do you know about your partners' lives? What do they know about yours? What is your reaction to knowing and sharing more? Since long-term relationships can thrive on the personal, you will likely need to share more of your life than your work would require. A deeper partnership often includes elements that are definitely outside the work role. And yes, learning more about each others' lives not only deepens the partnership, but complicates it. Consider whether you like your partners. Can you imagine being friends with them? Are you open to that possibility? Caring and friendship (not to mention love) are still difficult concepts in many work settings. I am not suggesting that you start inviting all of your partners over to the house for dinner, but there are benefits of having partners you like—especially when thinking about building long-term work partnerships. Though not essential, it is a great addition.

If you doubt the importance of developing this softer side of business partnerships, consider the option pragmatically: If much of your work is about change, you are about helping others let go of what is familiar in favor of something different. Change requires risk for those changing. People are more willing to risk when they trust the people supporting change, and that would be you. Trust springs from doing things together successfully through time, and that is what successful partnerships are all about. So it makes sense to develop relationships with key people in which you and they succeed by building on the trust you have nurtured together.

Whether your partnership is with a co-worker, your spouse, at the bridge table, or on a virtual team, be the partner you want others to be. Make yourself an attractive person to work with and get out there where others can see and choose you. The rewards of a fine partnership among capable individuals are really special; succeed at this a few times and you will know better what you are looking for the next time around. There is nothing quite like joining with others to complete a task, building on each others' talents, accomplishing goals, and savoring the experience. To partner well, *you* are the place to start because you bring yourself to every partnership you will ever participate in. Those other key people are not here right now: You are! And you can do something about yourself when you choose. Learn about partnering by doing it; pay attention to the quality of your partnerships. Reflect on your experience working with others: What works in your particular situation? Look at what you have learned about partnership in friendships, in marriage, in social activities, in civic organizations, and keep track of your learning.

The Golden Rule is a great foundation for all partnerships. Take it seriously: "Do unto others as you would have them do unto you." Said another way, show others how you want them to work with you by the way you work with them. They are learning from your actions. When you listen to them, they are more likely to listen to you. When you trust them, they are more likely to trust you. When you are willing to risk and act, they will be more willing. So, take the initiative! Whatever you want from them, do it for them first.

CHAPTER ELEVEN

Controlling Work Dynamics

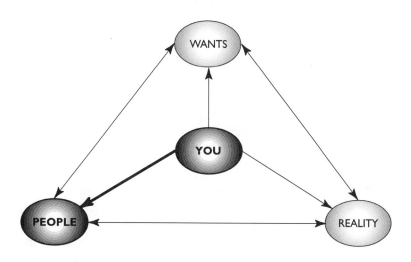

While building your relationship web, you will notice the strands vary in strength and density according to the relationships you have with people—and not all of this is intentional. Your connection to others is affected by the organization-sanctioned roles you all have. When you take on a formal responsibility that affects others, they deal differently with you. When you have some authority, and can make decisions that involve them, they will treat you differently and you will treat them differently.

This chapter is about those parts of your work where you do have some control, where others are expected to seek you out and get your support. In other words, they come to you partly because they are expected to. They "have to," and, you hope, they also "want to." Many staff, service, and support functions in organizations find themselves in this position—for example, when the human resource department reviews personnel decisions and when the comptroller signs the checks. The responsibilities that come with the role affect how the people in those roles are seen. We will look at those dynamics by putting you into this matrix:

A Model for Working with You

	Don't Have To	Have To
Want To	**Attraction**	**Acceptance**
Don't Want To	**Absence**	**Reluctance**

Put simply, the key people you work with *have to* work with you and/or they *want to* work with you—or they don't—and that results in different dynamics for each quadrant of the matrix:

- **ABSENCE:** *Don't have to and don't want to.* This quadrant of the matrix is not as negative as it might appear. When someone doesn't have to or want to work with you, you are not necessarily an awful person. You and this person are just not a work priority for each other; you each have other things to do if this defines both sides of your relationship. Since you do not have work in common, the social side will more likely define what you do together. Do not worry a lot about this quadrant where mutual work needs are ABSENT; save your energy for the other three quadrants.

- **RELUCTANCE:** *Have to and don't want to.* When you have a role defined by the rules of the organization, others may be required to deal with you. If they follow the rules, there will usually be some who resent the rules or resent you. What can you tell others to do, expecting they will listen and act? What can you expect they will do because you have the right to expect it of them? What is your recognized authority with other people? Your authority stems from the organization itself and somebody else probably made these rules and your role. You work within this authority—and beyond it, as you shape the role to fit yourself.

  This legitimate source of authority may have been captured in procedural manuals written years ago, or decided at the last meeting of your committee. The key to it, for our purposes, is that it comes from beyond you, and people in the organization are affected by it. It is legitimate for you to call upon the power of this authority, just as legitimate as calling on your expertise, which is another form of power. That does not mean others will like it. Think about what you have to offer them that they want, rather than reminding them that they have no alternative but to deal with you. Remember the source of your authority: It does not come from you, but from your position. When someone else has no choice but to deal with you, you also have no choice. This position of power and authority has its downside. I have noticed managers who begin to feel resentful of the very people who have come to depend on them—even when the manager encouraged their dependence. Those managers get caught in their own trap of expecting others to depend on them; they often feel overworked, blamed for the situation, and under-recognized.

- ***ATTRACTION:*** *Want to and don't have to.* Some people seek you out because they want to. They do not show up because agency policy #168A tells them to. They are not even there because their boss sent them. They show up because they see you as a resource. They want to use your expertise or influence or perspective. Maintaining a good work relationship with them is dependent on their taking away something they value, not on your authority. Working well with these people who are attracted to you is an excellent way of building a positive reputation in the organization while contributing to it.

  When the focus is on your usefulness rather than your authority, your individual skills are critical to how much and how often you are used. When people are not aware of your skills, they won't call. When they do know and work with you, you know that they are choosing to be with you; there is no regulatory coercion. You are dealt with more positively because of what you have to offer, and everyone has more control of whether this work, and working relationship, will continue.

- ***ACCEPTANCE:*** *Want to and have to.* Aim to get all "have to's" into this quadrant—not just those who are willing. "Have to" can be the basis for starting a work relationship, but need not define how the relationship develops. One approach is to build on the benefit of the "have to." For example, "Policy requires that we work together on this . . . Now, how could we build on that expectation in a way that benefits each of us, and the organization?" Emphasizing the "have to" of the job can squelch good relationships before they have a chance to begin. Even in controlling functions like accounting and finance, there is nothing in the rules saying you have to be officious, authoritarian, or mean. We will be effective, or not, as a result of a combination of our authority, our expertise, and our interpersonal skills. We usually cannot succeed based on our "have to" authority alone. "Want to and have to" work relationships have a special magic. They are supported by the organization; the situation requires that the people involved meet regularly to support something important to the larger organization; the people involved are motivated to do something together. There is a lot to be said for this ACCEPTANCE quadrant of the matrix.

Our Need to Control

Some people in those organizationally sanctioned positions of authority have a need to control; we all know—and many of us are—control freaks. Those readers who have *no* need to control others or outcomes can skip this section. The rest of us would do well to read it. Our need to control can come from our investment in the project we are working on, coupled with our impatience with the time it is taking to get the work done. Or, our certainty that we know how to do this better than others and the reality that training someone else to do this will take too much time. Or, we may have a great respect for people in authority and like being one—something we valued from early in life. And these human, not horrible, reasons deliver results each day across the world. The question is whether these reasons support continued individual and organizational effectiveness. Often, they do not.

So what are we controlling folk to do? Here is an array of ideas: Try sorting people you work with into the "have to/want to" matrix. Talk with those people about how you work with them right now: What works for them and what does not? How could you help some people move from "have to and don't want to" to "have to and want to"? Or, consider what you formally and informally control right now: Notice which controls you possess that are vital for the survival of the organization, compared to those controls that are vital only for your survival in the manner to which you have grown accustomed. What does that tell you about yourself? Ask others how you might move more control in their direction. Invite them to look more deeply at the work you have been holding to yourself, with the idea of passing some of it on.

Remind yourself of how little you can do in this organization by yourself; you depend on others to get things done. You are most effective when others help get the results you want and least effective when you do it all yourself. Believe this deeply; act on it daily. Remember the old Chinese proverb about teaching your neighbor to fish rather than giving him a fish each day. Do not exhaust yourself fishing, or building a huge fishing fleet, or developing fish markets. Instead, teach others how to fish. Seek opportunities to move control to members of the organizations you serve. Start with the assumption that putting control into the hands of those who are responsible for action will be best for the organization in the long run. Stay with this assumption until it has been proved wrong.

When others are not yet ready to handle work, get them ready to handle it; do not make their work part of your own. If they can't or won't get ready, question whether anyone ought to be doing this work. When people complain that they cannot move ahead because they are waiting for you, something is wrong. Your long-term effectiveness comes from preparing others to do what you now do. This perspective assumes people other than yourself have present abilities and real potential. You are called upon to trust that they will act in the organization's best interests. Trust that it's going to turn out okay—even if you aren't there to watch or guide every action . . . or . . . maybe *because* you aren't there to guide every action. No, you will not always be rewarded with outstanding performance. Yes, some important matters will slip between the cracks. And yes, the organization will be more effective than if you insisted on doing it all yourself.

Controls and controlling are important; your controlling side can serve you well. We must simply be careful that we don't hold our work so tightly that we squeeze the life out of it for ourselves and others.

CHAPTER TWELVE

Dealing with Decision Makers

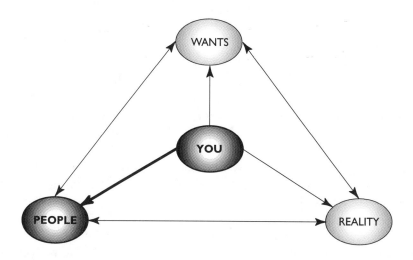

Those individuals and groups of PEOPLE that YOU work with include a category that many of us find troubling. They carry labels like "boss," "management," "the board," "executive," "the chair," and "leader." Whatever we call them, we recognize they have power in the organization—like it or not. And being part of this place means acknowledging that power. This chapter is about dealing with those people whose power you need to get things done. What they have in common is their responsibility to make decisions for the organization about work—including yours.

Just what works with these people? How can you gain their support to assure your success? My answers to these questions share one disturbing characteristic: Respect for their role and authority. I say "disturbing" because my answers bother *me*—especially when taken out of context. Know that I am trying to open your options; I am searching for more ways to help you succeed; and, as I make the case for the decision makers, I encourage you to understand them more deeply so you will be more successful with them.

One of the greatest mistakes we can make is to demonize the

decision makers in our organizations. I know, some of them deserve it, but let them earn that characterization rather than starting with the assumption that they deserve it. I have seen many bright and potentially effective people ruin their own chances for success by "knowing" in advance how awful the decision makers must be. This puts those bright people on the wrong path and reduces their options prematurely. Notice your own bias for and against authority. It deeply affects your thinking and behavior.

Show and Earn Respect

What do you say to co-workers about key decision makers in your organization. What do you say to your friends about your leaders? Can you detect any patterns of respect or disrespect in how you refer to those people? No, you do not need to respect every decision maker with whom you work. Some deserve the disrespect you give them, and others deserve the respect. My point has less to do with their worthiness and more to do with the consequences for you of feeling respect or disrespect toward them. Assume that whatever your underlying feeling, eventually they will know it. You will not be duplicitous or clever enough to hide disrespect for years. They will know that something is askew. And, worse yet, you will spend a long time presenting yourself as someone you are not. This next exercise suggests a way of dealing with your struggle. No guarantee, but it can open options for you.

AN EXERCISE

Building Respect

Often our lack of respect for another person grows from how they treat us or others. What constructive action might you take when you lack respect for one of those key decision makers?

1. Name one for whom you have less respect because of the way they treat you and others.

2. Consider why they are important to you and what you want from them.

3. What do they do now that bothers you, detracts from your respect for them?

4. What would you have them say and do if you could change them?

5. *NOW*—*and here is the leap*—What if *you* were to make those same kinds of statements and take those same kinds of actions that you set out for them in step four?

Yes, this is a five-step version of "Do unto others as you would have them do unto you." But do it first! When we get trapped in our negative perceptions of others, we narrow our sight and reduce our options at the same time. We begin to hold others accountable to our personal standards and we do not share those standards with them. We judge them harshly and they cannot do anything about it because we have not told them what is wrong.

You earn others' respect by taking actions that *they* respect—and that might be different from actions that *you* would first come up with if you wanted to gain their respect. But do the actions they would respect conflict with your values? Would those actions cause you to be untrue to yourself? Or, are the actions just different, unfamiliar, or uncomfortable? Consider doing it and discovering what it might gain for you. If you are hesitating, think again about what you silently expected of that person in step number four above . . . and then move again to step five, which tests whether you are willing to be as flexible as you want them to be.

An example from childhood comes to mind. My grandmother loved tea and cookies, and she loved to read the tea leaves in the bottom of the cup. As a ten-year-old boy, I was not the least interested in any of this, but I did love my grandmother. She would invite me to tea, complete with china cups. We were supposed to do this properly and I was supposed to learn how to behave. I earned my grandmother's respect by behaving in ways important to her; I also learned tea etiquette that serves me even today. And most important, because I was willing to do this, I had good conversations with my grandmother and we built a deep relationship over tea. If I had behaved entirely in my own ten-year-old boy's ways of getting respect, none of this would have happened.

Here is a work example. A software developer labored under a detail-oriented program manager. To meet the manager's needs, the developer documented his work at much greater length than he preferred. When the developer tried his more-casual approach, he was told he "needed more professional development." This comment irritated him and put some distance between him and the program manager. After he calmed down, the software developer used the five steps to assess his situation: He decided to do his work more like the program manager wanted. This meant letting go of his more informal approach and giving the program manager more detail. The results? More up-front documentation work for the developer—and more learning that came with that approach, including patience. Eventually, he began to appreciate the value of this approach. He noticed that there were fewer down-the-road challenges to his work. He was even praised by the program manager for his willingness to adapt and learn. Respect grew between the two of them. No, he did not become as detail-oriented as his boss, but he did learn how to do the detail, and he thinks that contributes to a better working environment for both of them.

They Don't Understand Your Work

That's true. Key decision makers often lack the deep knowledge and appreciation of your work that you would like them to have—especially if their role is quite different from yours. They are busy trying to understand their own work. But, if they only understood your work, you say, it would make a huge, positive difference. Without that understanding, they get it partly wrong. If they would just pay more attention to the details that they expect you to handle! These are common complaints expressed as our projects move up levels of the hierarchy to key decision makers. They are valid complaints, and with negative consequences. But . . .

Do *we* understand? Do we understand as much about *their* jobs as we are expecting them to understand about *ours*? Do we know the current organizational worries they are carrying? Do we know what goes into that bottom line they watch so closely? Can we interpret financial data or a production report? Do we know the pressure of leading an ever-changing organization in a chaotic world? Many of us are asking more of our decision makers than we are willing to deliver ourselves.

We are asking too much when we expect them to know every function with which they interact as thoroughly as those of us who are performing the functions. And they are asking too much of us when they expect us to be able to see their job as they see it. Each of us should reach out toward the other much more than we typically do. Since I am writing to you—and not those decision makers—I am asking you to initiate reaching out toward them. Learn more about their side of the organization. It is good for you and good for them.

Understand Their Purpose and Viewpoint

Has anyone ever implied that you don't appreciate what your organization is really about, that you are missing the larger point? And, have you ever reacted with "I know how this place works better than you think I do!" This is a common undertone of exchanges between the decision makers and the decision recommenders. Their respective views come with their roles. From the recommender's viewpoint, we feel under-appreciated, and our path out of this feeling is to use some version of the five steps discussed above: Demonstrate in expressed thought, feeling, and action that you get their point. Success is when *they* say you get their point—not when you say it. Of course, it would be nice if they did the same toward you, but don't count on it.

These key decision makers have their own perception of how well you understand this organization and their viewpoint. They "know," and they call up this impression every time you talk with them. They use it to guide how they deal with you, to gauge how much trust to place in you, and to determine whether you really have their best interests at heart. Think of a key decision maker with whom you work: What is their impression of you? How do you know? What have they told you? How could you find out more? What could you do to reinforce their impression? What could you do to alter it?

Do Not Wait: Initiate!

Recall conversations in which you heard someone say something like "If our team leader would just tell us what he really expects of us!" Or, "The Board just won't say what they want done!" Or, "If she would just tell us, we'd be glad to do it!" For me, these are familiar, and disempowering, words. What do they imply about who knows best? About who is at fault? About who ought to take action? The underlying assumption seems to be "Management should know all about how to run this organization; their role is to tell us; our role is to do it. They are not telling us, so we cannot do it." For some of us, this describes accurately how we want to work with the management of our organization. Others of us cannot accept this as the reality.

Another approach to these key decision makers puts us in a more powerful, initiating role. Instead of assuming their knowledge and waiting for direction, we assume our knowledge and take action. In this perspective, we are the focal point for knowledge, expertise, and action. We expect less guidance because the key decision makers know we are closer to the action and have a better understanding about what needs to be done. As long as we are making assumptions, why not make those that make us more powerful and effective.

Do not wait to be called upon. You *cannot* wait to be called on if you are to be effective. There is too much going on in organizations today for us to await the guidance of others. If you find yourself in an organization that withholds the information and/or resources you need to do your work, seriously consider finding another place to invest your talents. The pace of change requires organizations to structure themselves so members can respond to the opportunities of the moment. When that is not happening for you, test the limits of the organization; push it for what you need to succeed, for them and for yourself. If that doesn't work, leave. I do not want pessimists and cynics to use this as their escape paragraph. I think each of us must try repeatedly before giving up and moving on. And, we must try in ways respected by the successful people of the organization. And, there are limits.

Link Your Work to Key Systems

What are the organization-wide systems that key decision makers follow? What do these systems measure regularly? Look at the relationship between these priority systems and your work. How are they connected, or how could they be connected? How could your function and work become part of the key systems?

Here's an example that will be familiar to many readers. The planning/budgeting system is in place and working in many organizations. You may participate in it now, adding your input about your intentions and needs for the coming year. Let's assume that you have to provide your input by mid-September, like everyone else. What could you do two months before, in mid-July, that would help others you work with to prepare their plans? How could you help them plan *their* work with *your* work in mind? What could you do to influence others early in their planning? If you tracked capital expenditures, you could send people a listing of this year's expenditures in a format that aids them in preparing for next year. If you were in human resources, you could compare this year's movement of people against projections in the strategic plan and recommend actions for the upcoming planning period. A trainer could project online and workshop training, send it out to the organization, helping all managers plan for the coming year. These are ways of linking into key systems valued by others.

Seek Reviews of Your Work

Expect to be held accountable for what you do. Demand it. Too many of us avoid being evaluated by the organization. We say "They wouldn't understand what I'm doing" or, "What if they don't like what they see?" We fear they will take drastic action—such as dropping our favorite project—so we are overly protective. In doing this, we distance the decision makers from what we do and maintain their ignorance of it. This can lead to just what we feared: Decisions made by people who do not understand what we do.

Organizations try to track what is important to them: What and who do they track in your organization? How do they do it? Are they tracking your work? What should they be tracking of what you produce, considering your impact on the organization? As difficult as it is to be held accountable by people in authority and outside your control, that is exactly what you should pursue.

When was the last time you sat down with the key decision makers in your work and life to talk about what you are doing? When did you last meet with the chair of that important committee, or your spouse, or your board, or your boss? If you have been doing this, you know the value. If you have not been doing this, think about the opportunity you may be missing. Consider: What could be the value to you? To the other party? To the organization?

Meet with key decision makers at least twice a year to talk with them about what you are doing, how you are doing it, and what you might do next. In the process, you will learn a lot from each other about your roles and how you support each other. And your partnership will grow. And the organization—whether a civic club, a company, or a marriage—will benefit. Doing this for the sake of your ego is not a good enough reason. Take an organizational perspective on it. Will this meeting help all involved carry out their roles better? Will they learn from the meeting? Will the meeting affect what happens next? There are many potential rewards to these reviews. You can educate others on what you do by informing them of what you have done since the last time you met. You can put forth your priorities for what's next, seeking their agreement or alteration of your priorities. You can seek their priorities and show how your work supports them. And, you can appreciate their partnership and support.

With all these possible advantages come a few risks, starting with just being open with them about your assessment of yourself, your real hopes and concerns. And, you may discover that this particular decision maker is not getting what they want from you. This can be hard to handle, even though it is useful to know. Their own needs and questions may take you away from where you wanted to go; your meeting might be useful, but not in the way you intended. Put these risks beside the opportunities and decide whether you want these meetings or not. The meetings can be the foundation for a solid partnership with people whose resources and commitment you need.

Find Ways to Offer Feedback

Sometimes your effectiveness is tied to a key decision maker who is not that effective. It is often the case that no one has talked with them about it. Recall the times that you and others have discussed a decision maker's ineffective behavior, but not told the key person anything about it. What happens? Typically, those of us who were part of the discussion are reinforced in our beliefs. The decision maker continues in her same old ways because she does not know any better. And those of us observing her judge even more harshly because of what we know together. When you choose not to put the issue before her, you are part of the silent conspiracy to that supports her being less successful. You may make this legitimate choice; it may be the best way to go, but how much sense does it make to withhold information from others and then blame them? Only a serious threat would justify doing this. When the punishments we imagine have a basis in experience, withholding can be the best route.

There are more effective paths never considered—paths that involve getting feedback to the decision maker and opening their options. The first steps on this path are the trickiest. Here are some ways of getting feedback to a person whose behavior negatively affects your work and the work of others:

- *Tell them.* No, don't just sit down and spill it all out, but build your relationship to the point that you can talk about how you each approach your work.

- Ask the person for feedback on your own work behavior. When that works, check out whether they would be interested in flipping the process, getting input from you.

- Tell the person that you want to talk with them about how they approach their work, but you do not feel safe doing so yet. Talk with them about what would allow you to feel safe—with the intent of finding enough safety to open up to them. If you cannot find this safety, do not do it.

- Talk with others you work with about sharing the feedback with the key person. Search for an option that would work for all of you.

- Bring together your work group to talk about what you produce and how you produce it. List what you currently do well and not so well, what you could do better. This is when the data related to the key person would come out. Then agree together on what you will do, with everybody agreeing to something.

- The group could write a letter to the key person. Express in specific terms the wonderful and effective things they do. Express your concerns as specifically—but not as lengthily. Give it to the person, do not mail it. Express the group's willingness to talk about it.

- Use an outside consultant to gather information on the effectiveness of this work group, including the key person but also everyone else who is part of the work. Together, meet with the consultant to work through the report.

- Encourage the key person to ask someone else to help them think about how they approach their work. A personal coach or counselor might be a good idea. Introduce the idea in a highly constructive fashion accepting that we all need help in learning to do our work.

If you had a specific person in mind, you may have gone through the above ideas looking for an option that could work for you. I hope my ideas helped, but there is a good chance that you will have to come up with your own option in the spirit of my ideas. Do not get discouraged;

do not give up too soon. For your own sake, for the sake of co-workers, and for the sake of the organization, search for ways of making this troublesome person into a better contributor. Find a constructive way of getting your thoughts on the table.*

This chapter's main points suggest the potential for partnership with key people in your organization. Few of us like it when others regularly make decisions that affect us without hearing from us. We want to be involved if it affects us. And we understand that organizational realities can preclude that. But somewhere between no involvement and total involvement lies the relationship you can build with key decision makers. Using ideas like those I've suggested, you can build informed, productive relationships with the key people in your work and life.

---

*For some excellent help on this dilemma, see *The Courageous Messenger: How to Successfully Speak Up at Work,* by Kathleen Ryan, Dan Oestreich, and George Orr. Berrett-Koehler, San Francisco. 1996.

CHAPTER THIRTEEN

How Might You Help?

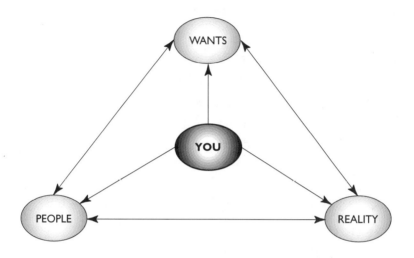

The GTD model puts YOU at the center of the action. WANTS, REAL-ITY, and PEOPLE connect to YOU—and often YOU connect them with each other, keeping them from functioning as separate elements. When you lead, others can choose to pursue meaning, to face the truth, to use their talent. YOU offer that opportunity. Or, you may not. Which leads to the focal question "How might you help?" Though this chapter affirms the power available to you from where you sit in your organization, you do not have to do everything. Use yourself judiciously; always consider the possibility that you might not be needed here. With that caution, let's proceed.

You don't have to be in charge of the world, or the department, to take charge of your life and your roles in organizations. When you free yourself of the notion that position is the ultimate authority, you can open to discovering the many other powers at your disposal. When you believe that you are uniquely positioned to accomplish something, you can set out to discover just what that something might be. Capitalizing on your position in the middle of an organization is not easy, but it is full of challenge and growth.

Take the lead in your life if you are to have any reasonable hope of getting what you want. Otherwise you depend on good fortune and the support of others to get what you want, and that is quite a gamble. Leading your life is completing the GTD model within yourself, linking YOU with your WANTS, your REALITY, and your PEOPLE. Connect the dots and activate the current. Discover and transform yourself.

The upcoming chapters are all about leading your own life while working with others. YOU are the focus: your leadership, your power, your courage, and your reward. These chapters are more personal, in that *you* are the focus rather than the organization. The questions you have asked of the organization are now turned in your direction. In terms of the GTD Model:

WANTS
What do you want from your life?
What do you want from the work you do in your life?
How would others describe what you want?
How does their description fit with yours?
How committed are they to supporting you in your wants?

REALITY
How would you describe your life as it is right now?
How would you describe the work part of your life right now?
How responsible do you feel for the current state of your life?
How would others describe your life right now?
How do their descriptions fit with yours?
How committed are they to supporting your life as it is?

PEOPLE
Who are the key people in your life?
Who could be affected by changes you want to make?
What are their special talents, resources, or powers?
What power do they assign to you?
How willing are they to work with you?

YOU
What special talents, resources, or powers do you have?
How are you currently using those abilities?
How might you use those abilities?
What do you care about changing in your life?

All of these questions suggest deep thought and solitary work, necessary if you want to empower yourself in your life and work. The organizations we work with spend hours reinforcing what they are about; they are often quite clear about what they want. You will not likely stand up well against all that power and focus unless you bring some of your own from outside the walls of the organization you serve.

AN EXERCISE

Self Discovery

Most of us need help reminding ourselves what is important to us. This exercise is designed to do that. It takes about three hours, over two months.

1. Make an appointment with yourself; put it on your calendar. Set aside 30 to 60 minutes of quiet time to answer the above questions on WANTS, REALITY, PEOPLE, and YOU. Answer as many as you can.

2. During your appointment, write down your responses so that you can return to them later.

3. Schedule another 30 minutes at least a week from now to return to these questions and your answers.

4. In the meantime, talk with someone important to you about what you have written so far. Get their reactions.

5. During your second appointment, review your earlier responses, consider what you heard from others, and answer any other questions you have time for.

6. Schedule a third appointment with yourself about two weeks out. Repeat the cycle completed in steps one through five for as long as this is useful to you. Search out other actions you could take that will reinforce your clarity of life purpose. For example, talk with more key people about your life, and/or read related books.

This exercise usually yields some significant discoveries or deeper insights or renewed commitments to some parts of your life. The questions and your answers anchor all that you do in your work. If *there is a secret to getting things done when you are not in charge, it is being deeply anchored in your life.* You succeed better in life *and* work because work is tethered to your life anchor. The underlying theme of this book is about life—though it talks about work. From the beginning, I talked about the work game as a part of your life game rather than the other way around. In the work game you are not in charge; in the life game, you are. Your power comes from knowing which game must prevail, which game must be won. Reminding yourself of your life game is your primary source of power.

Leading, in your life and work, requires going places you have never been. Leading will require that you separate yourself from others. Leading will ask you to express yourself so as to attract others to you. Your leadership will help others realize what they want and how to take responsibility for getting it. The rewards of leading will come primarily from within yourself. And, you will have to remind yourself that when you choose not to lead your life, others will lead it for you.

Leading combines visualizing what you want with sorting out what is and doing something about it. Without action toward your vision, you are less of a leader—of your own life or anyone else's. When you have a vision of what you want, you see the world through that vision; you look constantly for opportunities that might allow you to move reality closer to your vision. When you lead well, others understand and value your ideas. They sign up for doing what you and they want to do. You do not always have to speak with words; often actions suffice. The vision you share may be as large as a world at peace or as small as contributing to a more productive workplace, but whatever it is must have meaning to your potential followers. They must believe in your ability to move them toward what you envision, and they must believe that they can help to bring the vision closer to reality.

I vs. They

Consider these statements: "I have not done it" or, "I don't think they should do it" or, "I don't believe I could do it" or, "I don't want to do it." Each of these statements contain an element of personal responsibility that does not use what others have done as an excuse. Contrast those statements with: "They shouldn't even try to participate in decisions" or, "Nobody around here could ever do that" or, "They would never let us get involved." These statements assign responsibility for actions to some higher authority. The "I" statements are replaced by "they" statements; personal responsibility is not evident. Notice the difference between the two sets of statements. Put aside any judgments about the truth of the statements. Focus on the difference between saying "I have not . . ." and "They would never let us . . . ."

The perspective is entirely different, isn't it? "I" statements allow me to be in control; I am choosing what I will do and I am aware of my choice. "They" statements assume *their* power and my subordinance to it. "They" statements put the focus outside myself and make me dependent on them. Generalizations ("They would never . . .") also take the focus off me and move it to the amorphous "they." This weakens me in relation to the outcome. It is a view that portrays me as smaller, less important, and less responsible. When I hold that view of myself, I limit my options; I blind myself to the array of possibilities that comes with seeing myself as someone with choices, with personal power.

Out There vs. In Here

Another powerful point: The important answers are not "out there;" they are "in here." We often ask what we can do to change and to become more effective. What course can we take? What book should we read? What are the three steps we need to follow? What are the right answers? All of these questions reflect a perspective that might be expressed as follows: "There are many people in this world who have learned before me. They possess knowledge and skills that would help me in my life. If I knew what they know, I would be more successful. The answers I need are out there somewhere." This approach has led many of us on searches "out there" for personal and professional growth. Though we have learned a lot from out there, we have not found all the answers we are searching for. Why? Because they are not all there.

Another approach involves an internal search that might be expressed in this way: "There are some parts of my thoughts, feelings, and spirit that I do not yet fully appreciate. If I learn more about that inner self, I can become a more aware and confident person; I could use my abilities more effectively. When I explore my inner self, I find there is much to learn. I have important and undiscovered answers still within me." This approach has also been central to many people in their personal and professional growth. Not all of the answers are in here, but it's an important place to look—especially when you consider your centrality to the GTD model.

Notice how the "answers are out there somewhere" approach ties to the "they are responsible" statements we were discussing earlier. It is easy to imagine someone saying to himself both "They would never let us . . . " and "The answer is out there somewhere, and they have it." Notice the dependence that comes with each of these statements. The individual ends up seeking answers out there in a world that somebody else controls, and playing a role in someone else's game.

And now, notice how the process of looking into yourself for knowledge ties to the "I am responsible" statements we were discussing earlier. Imagine someone saying both "I am choosing to . . . " and "There are answers within me." Notice the internal focus of both these statements and the independence that both statements assume. This individual is taking responsibility for her actions and growth, seeking answers from within. She is living a role in a game of her own design, playing by her rules, toward her purpose.

Do not read those last few paragraphs to mean that there is nothing to learn "out there," that all those organization games are irrelevant. Not true. But everything out there takes on new meaning when you bring it "in here" and consider it within your life and work purposes. The organization game becomes a part of the personal life game. And that empowers you.

Learning the Truth About Yourself

I am thinking about the people with whom I work. I often separate myself, stand back from them, and look at our organization and issues from a distance. From out here, I "know" what is needed; I "know" what our situation is; and I can see the gaps between our wants and our reality. I also see the contradictions, the paradoxes, the self-deception, the excuses, and the rationalizations we use to keep doing what we are doing and avoid doing what we say we want to do. It's maddening! It doesn't make any sense! It's stupid! I have said all of those things about my organization and wished I could change things! Perhaps you know those feelings too.

Dealing with the reality of our co-workers brings us face-to-face with a reality about ourselves—or at least it should. My co-workers are occasionally maddening and stupid and don't make any sense . . . just as I am occasionally maddening and stupid and don't make any sense. I become angry and frustrated with my own inability to be more consistent, to "walk my talk," to make my vision of myself a reality. And I carry this frustration with me. When I see co-workers not doing what I am also not doing, I take out my frustrations with myself on them. I only began to understand and accept this about myself within the last few years. I spent many more years thinking that my irritation was caused by those people "out there," with "them." Yes, there are problems "out there," but there are also others "in here." When I look at where my actions could have the greatest impact, where I have the greatest control, it sure ain't "out there." It's starts "in here" with me. I tell this story because I believe I am not the only person in the world facing these issues. How might the story apply to you?

Working with other people on accepting reality involves the harder work we have to do with ourselves. When we can understand, respect, and accept ourselves, we are better positioned to offer similar understanding to others. Usually they will feel more accepted too. They sense their kinship with us as we all work toward accepting ourselves and our organization.

Knowledge of Your Self

My primary source of my effectiveness is myself. Knowledge of myself is more important than the techniques and methods I have accumulated, more important than the many models and many years of work experience. After all the books I have read, the workshops I have attended, the years on the job, I return to where I started: Myself. My patterns of success with others have involved knowing who I am, what I want to do, what I believe in, what I aspire to. This knowledge gives me the confidence to propose and confront; the ability to know where I stand and to be honest about it; the openness to understand and respect others' needs in addition to my own. When I fail in my work, it is often because I literally did not know what I wanted, what I was trying to accomplish.

Here in this chapter focusing on YOU, we return to core human dilemmas and offer advice that sounds like what you might get from a self-help book, a life-skills workshop, or a counselor. Since there is so much of that help available elsewhere, I'll make just a few points. First, you are not through learning yet; you are still reaching toward your potential. You are an experienced, knowledgeable person part way through life. You have learned a lot and you have much to learn. Keep yourself open to what is to come. (This is a useful way of thinking about other people too.) Make regular efforts to understand yourself better. Use reading, workshops, the Internet, and friends to broaden your perspective. Reading this book is a good example—and at the back of it, in the Resources section, you will find other places to learn about yourself and your work. Find instruments and questionnaires that allow you to compare your scores to the thousands of other people who have been through the same materials. Learn about the differences in personality types or leadership styles or communications patterns. Find out how people with characteristics like yours have succeeded in the past.

Think about your work and why it is important to you. Consider what it has to do with your life's purpose. Find time each day to in some way (reading, meditation, solitude, journaling) remind yourself what is most important to you. If you don't, you will end up giving all of your time to what is important to others! Talk with other people about these matters. Find out why their work is important to them. Probe a bit to get beyond their surface thoughts. Thinking along these lines increases your self-awareness, and that will make you a more effective person, friend, or work partner. As you know yourself better, you will bring that to others and it will improve your relationships with them. You will contract more clearly; you will risk more readily; you will confront more appropriately; you will appreciate others more deeply.

CHAPTER FOURTEEN

Find the Courage to Risk

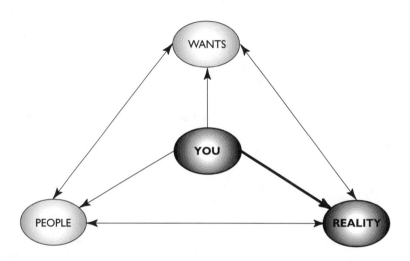

From the center of the GTD model, YOU are looking out in three directions as you reach for WANTS and enlist the support of PEOPLE. Since you want to *do something*, your fine considerations must be translated into action in the present, in the current REALITY. This calls for courage—the courage to risk, in the face of fears and opportunities. Answers to these questions support courageous action:

What do you want to happen now?

What are you willing to do to get it?

What are the risks?

Who needs to know about this?

What are you afraid of?

What arc your alternatives?

What will you do?

What have you got to gain?

What have you got to lose?

Can you live with the consequences?

These questions call out your inner choices involving opportunity and caution, risk and protection, courage and fear. Getting things done requires not just taking risks but, often, creating them. It means helping yourself and others step outside familiar boundaries. You help others move toward what they want by doing it first—and that is risky. You do this based on what you want and what you think others want. You see the organization as it could be, and you risk taking steps toward that imagined organization. The challenge is not in finding areas to change, but rather in taking the right risks to bring about changes accepted by the organization. Said differently, it is not so much *what* you want to change as *how* you go about it that requires courage and risk.

A company president was proudly showing me the new organization structure he had designed after hours of meetings among company executives. I was impressed by the structure and told him so. Yet I was skeptical of some of his selections for people to fill key roles in this structure. Having worked around this place for a long time, I knew the feelings of the workers. But he had not asked for my advice; he wanted recognition. While he enthusiastically put forth his plans, I was thinking, "I don't like some of this. Should I speak up? How should I go about this? What could I say that wouldn't hurt his feelings? Could this jeopardize my relationship with him? And, what will happen if I don't express my concerns?" I saw myself dealing with many of the questions listed earlier.

In his novel, *Something Happened*, Joseph Heller gives a telling, quantitative description of fear from the middle of a large organization.

> In the office in which I work there are five people of whom I am afraid. Each of these five people is afraid of four people (excluding overlaps), for a total of twenty, and each of these twenty people is afraid of six people, making a total of one hundred and twenty people who are feared by at least one person. Each of these one hundred and twenty people is afraid of the other one hundred and nineteen, and all of these one hundred and forty-five people are afraid of the twelve men at the top who helped found and build the company and now own and direct it.

Even though many of us work in organizations quite different from his, most of us know what Heller is talking about. We may experience the fear directly, or see it in others and deal with it through them. We see or feel the hesitation before moving forward. We see or feel the fear of losing something valued. We wonder whether others are trapped in a fearful response. Or, we identify with them. And we know the experience of putting more on the line than we intended.

The Risks of Stepping Forward

What do you risk when you speak out or take action on an issue in your organization? What are the negative possibilities that can cause you to clutch, perspire, worry, lie awake, hesitate, fumble, stutter, or make frequent trips to the restroom? What are you putting on the line that you fear you might lose? Look through these columns. See whether you have a pattern of worrying about losing . . .

Credibility	Neutrality
Job	Image
Money	Respect
Praise	Favor
Promotion	Reputation
Authority	Freedom
Privileges	Control
Power	Affection
Role	Time

Those of us who frequently feel at risk usually develop a pattern of worry. A friend talks repeatedly about her worry about getting fired for being too creative. Another worries regularly about how he will be seen by his bosses. Overcoming these fears calls for risk and courage.

The managing director of a local repertory theater has difficulty risking because she thinks her actions will cause people not to like her. As a result, in even small disagreements with her associates, she laughs a great deal and tries to get them to smile or laugh with her. She uses their smiles to assure her that they still like her. The truth is that liking/not liking her is seldom an issue. While they try to focus on the idea she has put before them, she keeps joking and laughing and taking them off the subject. When they seriously draw her back to the point, she uses their seriousness to tell herself that they do not like her . . . which causes her to try to get them to smile . . . which causes . . . This loop leads to a self-fulfilling prophecy in which the director ends up being liked less because her nervous actions get in the way of the work and lead others to like her less.

Finally, the director's associates took her to lunch and talked with her about their problems with her. She came away from that lunch understanding how her worries were getting in her way. She has now found other ways of assuring herself that colleagues like her; she is better able to make her points to them directly. People now say that they like working with her—just what she wanted in the first place.

Putting Fears in Perspective

Like the director, each of us brings some fear baggage to work with us. We picked up this baggage years ago—often in childhood—and we are still carrying it. These fears are not to be avoided but faced. It helps when we can be honest with ourselves about what we fear, rational and irrational. Just because we make it up it isn't any less real from our perspective. Think about the fears that haunt you, what you worry about in the middle of the night. Here are some common inner voices that speak from our fearful side; let's call them the great "What ifs . . . ." Are any of them yours?

What If I Get Fired?

If people were fired one-tenth as often as that fear crosses their minds, few of us would be left at work today. People are seldom fired for cause. It evokes images of our taking huge risks, laying ourselves on the line in the cause of high vision or values. It makes a good story with our friends over a drink. Our friends live through the harrowing experience as we retell it. They applaud our brave actions and go on to tell a story of their own about how they faced the organizational dragon and were nearly slain by it. We love those brave stories—like when I told of loving the bumps in Chapter 5.

"Organizational death," or getting fired, is *not* the worst thing that could happen to you. People who lose their jobs eventually find another and start fresh, often better off than they were before. The truth could be far worse . . . Worse than losing a job is *keeping* a job in which you are not respected, or not listened to, or not consulted, or not liked, or not influential, or . . . You name it; it's your fear. A recent study shows the four major fears of workers: loss of credibility or reputation, lack of career or financial advancement, possible damage to their relationship with their boss, and loss of employment (Ryan and Oestreich, 1991.) Our talk about fear of job loss is a cover; it places responsibility elsewhere—and it permits us to talk about fear at a less personal level. It is much easier to point at what others might do to me than to talk about what I really fear losing.

There are situations in which the fear is valid; you are truly in danger of losing your job. And you have no good alternatives. What might you do then? That is a good subject for another book, but here are a few ideas: Early on, check out the validity of your perception. When you are emotionally invested in an issue, recognize that your emotions will likely distort your perception; it might make sense to get someone else's assessment. Next, consider whether the potential firing is personal or situational. Are you being targeted as a person, or is this a general layoff where you are one of a number? Each case requires different steps. During a layoff, find out what is going on. Others are affected and there may be published information available. The best you can do is to be informed so you can move quickly—and remind yourself that this action is not because of your performance. You have few options within the organization.

On the other hand, if you are being targeted, you have more options. You can ask why; you can seek examples of what has happened that made you a target; you can seek other options. All of that is assuming some receptiveness on the part of the people targeting you. Though you are caught in an uncomfortable situation, you have more options because you are the target. What is the worst that could happen if you pursue some of these options? You might be fired—which you already anticipate. Your challenge is to invest your energy in pursuing creative options, rather than spending it in negative, immobilizing emotions. Avoid acting when you feel desperate.

The "big picture" guidance on the threat of job loss is keep your work game within your life game. When life is the greater game, you will use work in service to life. For example, you will have savings that could get you through lean financial times. And you will have built your personal power at work by being ready to leave if you must—while hoping that would not be necessary. The big answers to this big "what if . . . " are in your preparation long before the moment comes.

What If I Lose What I've Got?

Part of the frustration of change is that you must both give up something old and take on something new. Take the example of learning a new software package. You are reluctant to let go of the familiar because that's where your expertise, or at least your experience, is. And that is where your security is—sometimes even in situations that seem more negative than positive. There was a work group that had griped about its leader for as long as I had known them. Then one day, their (apparent) fondest wish was granted: The leader was transferred to a new location miles from the team. I expected elation, but what I heard was, "Now who will they stick us with?. . . We're going to have to break in somebody new . . . Will we all still be on the team?" When the old leader left, the team lost someone to talk about behind his back; they lost the predictability of his behavior and the camaraderie that came from joining together against him. And they were greeted by an uncertainty and insecurity that was more compelling for them than the positive possibilities a new leader might bring. Like that team, we should recognize that, with time, we become invested in what we have. Our familiar patterns provide security and do not like to be disrupted. The resulting discomfort is normal; we should live with it rather than try to get rid of it. It often helps to remind yourself that you have survived, and sometimes even thrived, during changes in the past. Move yourself to looking at what you have to gain rather than what you have to lose.

What If I Am Found Out?

Most of us have invested considerable energy in achieving our current position in life. Years of education and experience are behind the persona we display. On the other hand, many of us are aware of a significant difference between the self we put forward at work and the real self that stands in the background. Some of us are more proud of the image we project than the person who maintains that image. We have spent years constructing this image; we have worked so hard on it that we almost believe it. And the part of ourselves that is not consistent with the image lives in fear of being found out. "What if they learn that I am not the expert I pretend to be?" Or, "What if they discover that I have never done this before?" You may know what I am talking about. I am reminded of a fellow who wanted to impress a woman on their first date so he borrowed the fancy new car from a friend. The car did the trick; she loved it. And he told her it was his own. He then had to borrow that car for date after date in order to maintain the impression he made. This deception became a larger burden than he had imagined. He eventually "sold" the car on some excuse, and later married the woman. Much later, he owned up. I think some of us are driving cars that are not ours and we need to own up. We have to acknowledge both the facade and the fear of being found out.

What If I Get It Wrong?

I am here to confirm your worst fears: You *will* get it "wrong"—and probably quite often. We all get it wrong some of the time, and many of us have trouble accepting this in our reach for perfection or control. In our fast-paced world, there is no time to be perfect; the world will not stand still for it. The lesson is get it close, get it done fast, and adjust it as you go. This is not a prescription for sloppy work; it is learning to work with reality.

You may think it is your job to get it right. That depends on what "right" is. I don't think organizations keep us around to "get it right." We can focus too much on the expertise we bring and blind ourselves to the output the organization needs. What this place needs is usually far from what we would call "perfect." The people working around us do not want experts or perfectionists as much as they want contributors. To exaggerate: Accountants do not exist only to account, buyers do not exist only to buy, preachers do not exist solely to preach, and PR people do not exist just to PR. In the larger organizational perspective, we each exist to contribute in support of larger organizational goals. When we get caught up in our need to do it perfectly, we will get it wrong much of the time.

Expect to Miss the Mark

All of us get it "wrong" often; that is how we learn. Expect to be wrong often. Your recommendations will be appreciated, and not accepted as presented. Key decision makers, constituents, and others will like what you bring, and they will change it. Expect this to happen. This is part of being useful as others take ownership of some of your ideas. Expect to contribute, rather than to get it right. Notice when your work results in progress—even when what you offered was not fully used, or used in the way you intended.

Yes, there are other what-ifs; you could probably add a few of your own. Pay extra attention to the fears and anxieties that you return to often. Those patterns may be indications of something happening in your workplace, but they are more likely indications of something happening in you. You might ask yourself, "Why is it so important to me to keep returning to these fears?" It is an interesting question, with significant answers.

Building Your Courage: Three Exercises

Just as our body needs lifelong exercise, our heart builds courage through life preparation. We cannot plan on the exact moments we need to be courageous; we have to be ready. Our life is our preparation; we are as ready as we can be at this moment; life has prepared us to react. Since risk-taking and courage-building so often come up as issues, three exercises follow. Reading about risk and courage is not nearly as effective as doing something, so here's what you might try.

EXERCISE ONE

Willingness to Risk

Often it is not a question of whether we will risk, but how much we will risk. We are willing to put ourselves on the line for the sake of another or the organization, but how do we decide how much to put at risk? Here is a way that might help you sort this out:

1. Think of someone whose behavior you would like to change *and* whom you are afraid to confront.

2. Think about the magnitude of change you hope he would make.

3. How much risk would this be for him on a ten-point scale?

4. Risk as much as you would have him risk. Take action yourself, facing your risks and paralleling his risks. This will give you a sense of what he may be facing when he considers changing.

5. If you are not willing to risk at a level equal to your expectations of him, then lower your expectations of him. Ask no more of him than you are willing to ask of yourself.

Sorting Risk Responsibilities

This exercise asks you to reach beyond what *others* do into what *you* do that contributes to the discomfort in which you sometimes find yourself.

1. Picture a person with whom you find it intimidating to work.

2. Think about an important issue that you would like to put before this person.

3. Imagine yourself putting the issue before this person. How do you feel? Scribble down all the thoughts and feelings you would expect to have at that moment.

4. How would you like to feel at that moment? Scribble down all those thoughts and feelings, too.

5. Compare your answers from numbers three and four, the types of thoughts and feelings, the direction of the change from one list to the other, the overlap.

6. Now ask yourself what *the other person does* that causes you to feel as you do when you present an issue. Write these points down, noting everything you can that contributes significantly to how you feel.

7. Write down everything *you do* that causes you to feel *other* than the way you would like to at this difficult moment. What do you do that gets in the way of feeling better about yourself?

8. If number seven is hard to answer, consider these possible explanations:

- You are not doing anything that causes you to feel bad—it's all the other person's fault.

- You just haven't thought about it this way before and it takes a while to get on that wavelength.

- You have thought about it and know that this path leads nowhere, because even if you accept some responsibility, the other person still can control how you feel.

9. Based on what you now know, could you do something different that would positively affect your work with this person? When could you do this?

This is not to say that it is all your fault. No, you do not deserve everything bad that comes your way. But when it comes to changing behaviors, it is extremely difficult to change someone else. So start at the most practical place, with the person over whom you have the most control, the individual you most care about. Start with yourself.

Courageous Consequences

If you struggle with building the courage to confront issues, take 30 to 60 minutes to work through these steps:

1. Identify at least five situations in which you often feel at risk in your work. Describe each of them in terms of the present reality and what you want.

2. Consider the gaps between wants and reality in each of the five identified situations; search for patterns among the five situations. Then complete these two statements: "Overall, what I seem to want is..." or "Overall, the realities I face are . . . ." It would not be surprising if there is a pattern in the wants you have in these five situations. You may also notice that your five definitions of reality are related.

3. Now look at the five gaps between the current reality and the wants. What possible courageous actions could you take to close each of those gaps? Note them and look at the relationships between these actions in each of the five situations. They all call for you to be courageous; do they have more in common? Search for what they have in common; force a fit if you must.

4. Next, ask yourself "If I were to take these courageous actions, what repercussions could I face?" As you ask this, indulge your negative fantasies. Commonly, we fear that we will lose our jobs, we will be ostracized, we will be laughed at and rendered ineffective, or we will die. Whatever it is, write it down. Then read these notes aloud to yourself—with feeling!

5. Now, ask yourself "If I were to take these courageous actions, what good could come from it?" Consider what positive difference they could make to you, to the people around you, to the organization, to the world. Do this with all five situations. Write the possibilities down, then read your notes aloud—with feeling!

6. Remind yourself that this is an exercise in understanding your courage and fear, and you do not have to do anything about it that you do not want to do.

7. Talk with someone you trust who is outside the risky situations you have written about. Do not ask for advice; just tell her what you have been thinking about. Then ask her to tell you about similar situations in her life. Listen for similarities; notice how much or how little her thoughts fit with your own.

8. If the last step is rewarding for you, move on. If not, repeat it with another person.

9. Select one of the five situations that you might do something about. Now we are getting closer to action, but only if you want to. Decide on a small courageous action you could take that would represent different behavior for you.

10. If you really want to, take the action. Assess the result against what you have done in the earlier steps. Talk with the trusted person about the results.

Paradoxically, the best way to get around our fears may be by moving through them. Instead of avoiding our darker corners, moving toward them and bringing them out into the light can help. By looking at what we are afraid of, we can understand our fears better. We can anticipate situations in which a fear might arise and also avoid situations that we cannot handle as well as we would like because of our fears.

Influencing the direction of your organization means risk for you, whether you are saying what it ought to keep doing, or stop doing, or how it ought to change. Any of these actions requires defining who you are and where you stand. How do you know what your contribution is if you cannot identify what you have done? Can you point to what is happening differently because of you? What is your unique contribution? Making that difference requires risk and courage.

Courage and risk are present throughout our life and work experience—and the GTD model. The dynamics between you and the three corners of the model offer courage-building opportunities. Clarity about your vision of what you want increases the likelihood you will reach for it. Confidence in your understanding and appreciation of the current reality makes it more likely you will know how to risk. The support of key people in the organization adds to your power when you take action. Deep understanding of your abilities and limitations allows you to use yourself appropriately. Courage does not come from "out of the blue;" you prepare yourself to be courageous by attending to the four elements of the GTD model.

CHAPTER FIFTEEN

Making Your Work Rewarding

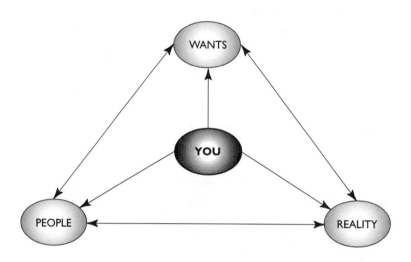

There are many possible rewards for doing your work well. Some unique combination of rewards attracts each of us. Consider what the items in these two columns have in common.

Promotion	Personal growth
Advancement	Sense of accomplishment
Pay increase	Professional satisfaction
Bonus	Self-reliance
Awards	Building your resume
Gifts	Making a unique contribution
Stock options	Moving toward your vision
Stature	Honoring your values
Wider recognition	Becoming a better person

These columns are sorted into two types of rewards. The rewards in the lefthand column are external; they are decided and bestowed by others and then given to you (you hope!). They can be wonderful to receive and they are outside your control. Someone else decides how you are performing; they judge you by the rules of their game. I like receiving these rewards; you probably do too. When others recognize our contribution to the organization, we feel affirmed. But we do not control the award, and that is a critical consequence of externally initiated rewards. The righthand column is filled with internal rewards. These come from within and are conferred by you. You reward yourself based on how you performed against what you value. You decide what qualifies you for the award and, when you meet those qualifications, you recognize yourself. You did it; you know it; you feel good about it. All of this is within the goals and roles of the "game" you are designing and playing. These internally initiated rewards are under our control, can be very fulfilling, but are often celebrated alone.

Internal rewards link tightly with the peak of the GTD model, rewards realized when you get some of what you want, and when you recognize that you have moved toward what is important in your life. When you are getting things done and you are not in charge, you look to the right column for your primary rewards, for your definition of success. Left column rewards are fine, but they are "icing on the cake;" the right column is "the cake." Go for the cake; accept the icing that comes with it.

The actual rewards of work cannot be sorted easily into two columns. For example, when you receive a bonus and are told that you earned it through your exceptional work this year, how does that feel? That external bonus pairs up with internal rewards of accomplishment and satisfaction, crossing over our tidy two columns. That happens frequently when external rewards come our way.

Creating your own rewards is the way to succeed in your work and life—especially if you are not in charge of the rewards out there in your organization. As wonderful as external rewards might be, they come from others and are unreliable—at least when compared to the rewards you can generate for yourself. I am not faulting others for attempting to entice you with their prizes; after all, we do the same toward others when we hold out external rewards for them. This is a cautionary reminder that external rewards can be both distracting and compelling.

Reaction and Reward

When we carry out our role in a dependent fashion, our rewards are at the option of others. Behaving dependently leaves decisions about our recognition in the hands of the people we depend upon. Our passive stance toward our work tends to put us at the mercy of those who are more active and have their own ideas about what we are doing. We are in the position of reacting to what they want in order to get what we want. A pro-active stance could make it more likely that we decide our own rewards.

Consider differences between being reactive and pro-active: They are as different as responding and initiating. As different as being called and stepping forward. As different as dependence and independence. As different as being patted on the head and patting yourself on the back. There is satisfaction available in doing what is expected and doing it well, but it is limited. Rewards increase dramatically when you initiate projects of your own. Tending to your work offers rewards quite different from joining with others to pursue an opportunity. The reward for answering others' questions differs markedly from the reward for putting forth recommendations. We all find rewards in both the reactive and pro-active arenas. Seek both, and know your balance. Organizations often emphasize the external rewards because that is easier for a system to do—not that most organizations do it all that well! You must emphasize moving toward your internal rewards if you want them.

The Rewards of Membership

In return for our commitment to serve, our organizations offer their resources, a place to work, a role, income, benefits, coworkers, a purpose, and a chance to influence. These rewards come so regularly as to be presumed; we deal with it all as "given" and forget about it. We keep working here for many reasons. One, the organization reliably delivers what we need. We stay here rather than trying to provide our same services on our own out in the marketplace. Two, we have talents and needs that require resources that one person cannot pull together. A large organization brings together the financing or equipment or technical teams needed to do what we want to do. Three, we find the larger world professionally lonely and join an organization for the companionship. Four, we like the discipline that the organization provides us.

We find it easier to work within its structures than to build our own. Five, we believe that the only way to get anything important done is through combining forces with other like-minded people in an organization of some sort. We cannot do it alone.

Yes, there are rewards for just being here. Rewards that play themselves out each time we go to the copy machine or the coffee machine, each time we stroll down the hall to visit a friend or search out an expert working in a nearby cubicle. Even when our experience nets out negative, we must factor in the daily rewards that we often take for granted.

Making Your Work Rewarding

You give lots of time and talent to serving your organization and the people in it. They are unlikely to give you the appreciation you deserve. You will be under-appreciated—just like they are. This is not to imply that others are heartless and uncaring. Well yes, a few are, but most mean well and simply don't give the recognition that people deserve. So, if you suffer from a lack of appreciation, there may be some small comfort in knowing this is a widespread ache. I'm not saying "Forget it; we all suffer." I am saying that organizations—especially large ones— have not succeeded in systematically recognizing human contribution. It's a work-in-progress in most agencies and companies, which is all the more reason to create rewards for yourself.

Finding rewards often requires looking in new and different places. Too often there is no one there to tell you how you are doing, where to look, whether you are "getting hot" or "getting cold"—as in the childhood game. Or, well-intentioned people guide you in directions that don't fit with what you want. At the risk of being yet another false guide, here are some ways to make your work more rewarding.

Tell others what you are doing and give them a chance to comment on it. This can be a wonderful source of reinforcement. Or, give others the recognition they are seeking and perhaps they will turn about to do the same for you. Or, take a longer-term, strategic perspective on the organization. Direct your efforts toward that larger tomorrow, not just what you are doing today. There are often rewards "out there" that you cannot see when focused "in here." Or, remind yourself that you are in service to the larger community and humankind, that this work is a way you contribute to life.

Remind yourself of what you want, your aspirations and values, and see how they fit with other people with whom you work; talk together about what you all receive from this work. Try collaborating with other people, opening yourself to the rewards of partnership and synergy. Form a web of key people and maintain the web through regular contact. Let go of your more competitive inclinations. Or, seek the people in your organization who have a positive approach to their work. Learn what they find rewarding. You can also seek out people in other organizations and trade ideas across boundaries. They understand your work and your dilemmas; they have faced similar issues. Talking with them will be rewarding to you all. And last of all, there are special rewards that come with training, counseling, or coaching others. You might try coaching more and playing less. Search out the satisfaction that can come from helping others learn.

These possible rewards do not come with guarantees; none of them offers immediately tangible results. They are right-column versus left-column rewards. What they lack in tangibility they make up for in control. You can do much more about putting these rewards in place. You will feel a certain power in acting on them. It may not feel like a raise or a public commendation, but it will feel good because you are doing something about getting what you want. All of the listed ideas encourage you to step back from your work and look at it from an expectant, positive, collaborative perspective. Daily work pressures may not encourage us to follow these ideas, but that does not invalidate them. Consider the rewards you now get and ask if they are enough. If they are, fine, stick with them. If not, take another look at the ideas I have offered.

Turn to yourself for appreciation, confirmation, affirmation, celebration, and all those other "-ations" you deserve. Others can support, but we provide our own best and most reliable recognition. We know what we want and how we want it; it's time to give it to ourselves. We also know when we deserve it and when we don't. Which reminds me . . .

Praise Fixation Breeds Dependence

Have you noticed how often the recognition you do get from others misses the mark? "He told me he really liked the three-ring binder design, but he didn't mention what's inside!" Or, "She said she really appreciated my finishing on time, but she didn't say a word about what I'd presented!" See what I mean? When they do it, they often do it "wrong"—wrong in the sense that it does not meet our specific need for recognition. They cannot recognize us on our own terms because they do not know what our own terms are. They would have to be there with us doing the work to deliver the appropriate praise we earned. We can write their lines more accurately and deliver them to ourselves more enthusiastically because *only we* know intimately how to recognize ourselves.

Those who praise are given power by the those of us who need the praise. This truth is more obvious when it comes to criticism; you know the power we give to the criticizer. The trick with praise is to accept it and not depend on it. Derive your primary satisfaction from meeting your own internal standards and supplement that satisfaction with what you receive from others. In more trying times, when others are not there to give you recognition and support, you will be stronger for having depended on yourself.

AN EXERCISE

Rewards from Your Work

Here is a chance to reconsider the rewards of your work in a more thoughtful way. Take 20 minutes of quiet time to think through these steps.

1. Assess how rewarding your work has been for you lately: What does it give you in return for all you put into it? How important are those rewards to you? For reminders of possible rewards, look back at the two columns at the beginning of this chapter.

2. Note those rewards you receive from others. How important are those rewards to you? How dependent on others do these rewards make you? How do you feel about that?

3. Note those rewards you receive from yourself. How important are these rewards to you? How satisfying are these rewards to you? How do you feel about that?

4. If you were to change the rewards you get from your job, how would you change them? How would these changes affect your dependence on, or independence from, others?

5. If you were to pursue new rewards, what new actions would be required of you? What would you have to do to get those positive consequences you hope for?

6. What would be the risk of taking those actions? For you? For others? How big a risk is it?

7. What actions are suggested by all this thinking? What do you want to do? What will you do?

If you are regularly uncomfortable with the rewards coming from your work, this exercise—and this chapter—might help. If you seem far from getting what you want, then prepare yourself to change *something!* A pattern of doing work that drains you more than rewards you is a losing pattern. Continuing on the path will only reinforce and deepen it. Try something new; change your approach; change your strategy.

CHAPTER SIXTEEN

Create Change

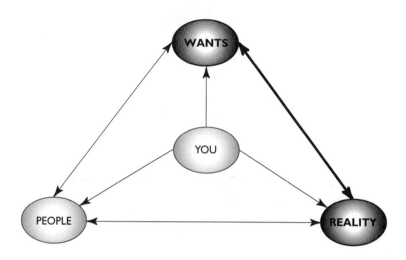

If we could devise a recipe for change, its main ingredients are shown in the GTD model: YOU and the key PEOPLE, their WANTS and the current REALITY. Yes, other herbs, spices, and ingredients can be added to bring out the flavor and consistency of the change you want, but without these four core ingredients, you cannot get the change you hunger for. And it is not simply a matter of throwing all the mixings into the organizational pot and stewing them together; it is much more subtle than that—and that is what this chapter is about. The focus is change, particularly on narrowing the gap between WANTS and REALITY. Yes, the YOU and PEOPLE will be involved, but this chapter is particularly concerned with the nature of change and what is involved in building a constructive tension between what you've got and what you want.

Stability Meets Instability

People working in organizations often are rewarded for creating stability; that's what organizations have been about through much of history.

Organizations assemble resources toward a common purpose within a structure to produce predictable outputs. No, it doesn't always work that way, but that is the intent. The important point is that they seek out the "best" way, find it, adopt it, and don't want to let go of it. And the members of the organization are rewarded for finding and maintaining this stability. Change is particularly difficult in this environment. Building a stable organization that is receptive to instability is a hard notion to grasp. It's possible, but when people do not understand that concept, they will resist the change rather than welcome it.

If your work requires considering and proposing improvements to your organization, you know the barriers you run up against—barriers that are part of the nature of organizations. As someone who intends to make some changes, you have tension built into your work with others. Service and support functions know what this is about. They are in business to build the best information, financial, knowledge, learning, or people systems. They are rewarded for building better systems, but that requires change among the users of their systems, and there is the rub. If you serve the organization in one of those functions, you know firsthand the resistance your work often provokes. Or, if you are a consultant to organizations intent on improving themselves. Or, if you are a citizen recommending changes in your community schools or government. In each of these cases, you step into the momentum of an organization that wants to move in stable and predictable ways.

When people receive your e-mails, or see you coming down the hall, their heartbeats do not necessarily quicken in anticipation of the wonderful new ideas you are bringing them. No, they have stability to serve and predictability to pursue; that's what they get rewarded for. Your support for new ways can push them to hold tightly to their old practices. If they let go, they may have to acknowledge that the stability they have been maintaining is less perfect than they imagined. Or, that their organization is not as wonderful as they claimed. Or, they might be taking on an enormous amount of work without the certainty of positive results. There are thousands of reasons to resist your enthusiasm for changing their work. Many of those reasons are valid; all of them deserve your respect.

There are many ways you can ensure their defensiveness—and your superiority. For example, you can imply that they are not that smart, that you know better, that you are right and they are wrong. But you do not need a lesson in how *not* to introduce change. How we go about introducing change is often more important than the change itself. Your great idea may never get a hearing if you present it in a way that makes people want to reject it, whatever it is.

The world tells us that we must change to get ahead, to keep up, even to stay in place. We need to be more than a function of other people's changes; we need to invest in it, lean into it, and help it happen. That is our best chance to get things done wherever we are in the organization. When we don't take the chance to affect change, others will, and we will be subject to changes we did not form. We will end up, in the extreme, victims of change rather than leaders of it.

The rest of this chapter offers a dozen considerations that can aid you in bringing about change. These points are based on the practical research of real-life experience. You can view them as principles to be followed, or see them as a checklist for your review during the change work you are doing. See these twelve expectations as a backdrop to the projects you are working on. They can shift your expectations going in, making you more receptive to, and accepting of, the problems you face along the way.

The Need for Change Must Be Compelling

Given what we face when we introduce change, we had better be clear in our minds and our hearts about what we want. Whether making a change in ourselves (exercise, catch up on work), or helping our work team change (better meetings), or working for change in our organization (new systems, respect for people), our clarity about what we want is our guiding star through the whole process. We will only be able to move forward through daily disruptions and distractions when we have a clear vision of what we want. Loss of the vision means loss of the focused energy necessary to something new. We will not die, but we will return to the status quo that we thought we were escaping. The vision of what we want must be so compelling that it inspires us daily; it affects our every decision.

As you think about the changes you want: How compelling are they? Do they consume your thought? Do they engage your energy and passion? Do they provide you with the power you need to move through the change, beginning to end? These questions demand strong affirmative responses. You do not want to run out of motivation midway.

Leading Change Is Demanding

Much is asked of us when we decide to change our lives and our organizations. Precedent will challenge our every action, whether it is our personal eating habits, or the voting habits of our precinct, or the way our civic club runs meetings. In each case, our new ideas come up against the momentum of precedent. Habits, norms, rules, values, procedures, history, and culture expect us to fall into their established patterns.

Do not overestimate your ability to bring about change, or underestimate the organization's ability to maintain itself. When we are less experienced in organizational life and steeped in our ideals, our naivete about how change happens is striking. Our assumptions lie at the extremes: "This organization will never change" (Despair! Despair!) or, "If they just changed this one policy, it would fix everything!" (Joy! Joy!). These extremes do happen, but most organizational change falls between these poles.

After working with hundreds of organizations, I am still astounded by the complexity of any radical organizational change—and how little I understand it. I have specialized in bringing about change and I still have much to learn. The people I work with are usually much newer to changing organizations than I. One of my roles continues to be slowing them down enough to cover all the bases necessary for effective change.

Expect organizational change to be demanding and difficult. If you see organizational change as a simple matter, look again. If you define change primarily in terms of what makes sense, be careful. If you disparage the resistance and feelings of the people involved, watch out. If you think and act like you know best, you may already be in trouble. On the other hand, if you see change as difficult, you will prepare for it more thoroughly. You will feel more confident when complications occur. You will understand complexity as part of the change package.

Change Is Rooted in Respect

Many of us work for organizations that have been around a long time. In some cases, generations; in others a few years. In all cases, the people there worked hard to make the organization what it is today. They invested their minds, hearts, and hands in making this organization work. Ignore that history at your peril; respect that history and you will increase your chances of success. Respecting the history does not mean liking it or endorsing it; it means respecting that these people did what they thought best and this is the result. Without that respect, forces will line up against the changes you propose; you will have to deal with an organization defending itself, setting up a destructive we–they dynamic that will waste energy and block progress. Change is possible without respect, but it ain't easy. Use this expectation to check yourself: Do you respect those people in the organization that you hope will change? How do you demonstrate your respect?

Help Others Hear Your Ideas

Having a good idea is one thing; getting it heard is another. Too many of us act as if there should be a direct link between our new idea and change in the organization. It doesn't work that way. Being part of an organization has the advantage of access to its resources. But there are a few keys to turn before those resources become available. When other people are in charge of those resources, we have to help them understand what we need from them and why. We must help them decide to apply their resources to our needs.

Do not expect your ideas to be accepted the first time around. Through a combination of legitimate organizational filters, petty politics, and inattention, most of the new ideas that come along do not make it to implementation. You cannot control what others will do when they receive your idea, but you can control how you present it. Before putting it forth, think about the reception you want it to receive. Who ought to hear this idea? What do you want people to say when they hear it? How could you make it more likely they will say that? What action are you intending for them to take after hearing your idea? What could you do to make it more likely they will do that?

Resistance Reveals Power

Success in creating change is rooted in respect for the resistance to it. Understanding and accepting this resistance requires such intimate knowledge of the resistance that we may throw up our hands, feel it is hopeless, give up. But blinding ourselves to the resistance by ignoring it and trying to run over it seldom works—especially for people without formal authority. Resistance to change demonstrates the power of the organization; that power needs to be understood and respected.

One of the primary ways an organization flexes its muscle is by opposing change. You may feel like avoiding or disparaging this resistance; you might try to roll over it. But if you are working with a large or old organization, you are more likely to be rolled upon. Listen to yourself and others. Listen for comments like "These people just do not understand" or, "They are holding onto outdated ways" or, "They are in trouble and don't know it." These comments may be clues that you need to learn more about the organization.

Perhaps "those" people really don't understand and need information. Don't blame them for not understanding something they have never had the opportunity to absorb. Perhaps they are holding onto outdated ways, but how would they describe what they are doing? And, how would they describe the "trouble" you think they are in? Do they know they are in trouble? Often our interpretation of resistance prevents us from picking up the clues that would lead us to deeper involvement with the very people who are resisting. Have these people been involved in developing the change? Have they influenced it?

What if you were in their shoes? How would it feel to be the "changee" rather than the "changer"? You have been there before; you know what it's like. Think about your reactions when an organization put expectations on you to change. Perhaps it was your employer, or the people you work with, or your family, or your community. Or educators, environmentalists, health care professionals, politicians. Notice your reactions as the changee; you can be sure that those reactions exist among the people you are asking to change.

Putting myself in that role as the target of change is not difficult. I feel its daily pressures. The sheer volume and intensity of the change being asked of me causes me to pause before committing myself to something new. I am not looking for opportunities to reach out and embrace something new. I grew up in a world that was much more predictable than the world that surrounds me today. I was raised expecting stability and I learned to value it. When you or the phone company or my computer network or my co-workers come to me with something new, my first inclination is to hold on to the stability I have spent years cultivating. I may react to your new ideas as a threat, avoid listening to them, and prepare to defend what I have. Your ideas are coming up against my habits, or something valued that I will not easily release. And I am someone who has changed a great deal in my work and my life—often reluctantly, sometimes willingly. My zeal for having others change is almost always greater than my zeal for changing myself.

That paragraph is full of clues about me. If you were to write your own paragraph about how you deal with change, what would it contain? Perhaps that would increase your empathy for the folks you are trying to move off dead center. And what would their paragraphs say? We each have personal boundaries that raise an alarm when trespassed. It is not so much a matter that some people are willing to change and others are not; it is more a matter of each of us raises the alarm.

Perseverance Required

Dreams and wants cannot be brought into reality overnight. Major change in individuals can take years of work, so what might it take to help an organization turn in a new direction? Do you have the energy to persevere in the long struggle? Are you willing to commit to what is required to succeed? And, what are your chances of success? These sobering considerations should occur early in undertaking any change effort because you can count on their coming up later when your work is challenged or the effort is flagging.

The easy, energizing, exciting part is coming up with the ideas for change, gaining support, getting approval. The hard part is what happens after the launch, after the excitement of starting fresh—implementing the change and making it an established part of "how we do things around here." Change must maintain itself over the long run and without continual energy transfusions from you and others. It must move ahead on its own momentum. For important changes in organizations, it takes months and years, not days or weeks, to reach this point.

Imagine that your organization wants to underline its belief in the importance of communicating with workers, and it chooses to do this through an intentional, thoughtful set of meetings for people who work together. In fact, it asks people to identify three key work relationships and then talk with each person about how they are doing together. The organization wants people to have these 1- to 2-hour discussions at least twice a year. That's it; that's the change. How long would it take to get this little system up and running in your organization? How many years before everyone understands the intent of these meetings and has the skills to hold them? How many years before these discussions are consistently held and valued? One year? Two years? Five? You know your organization and I don't, but I'd say at least five years in a large, multilevel, older organization.

That is just one easy-to-imagine example. It is not nearly as complex as many of the change projects circulating in organizations today. Consider what your expectations are in the change projects that engage you. Have you allowed time? How have you prepared to persevere? What do others around you expect? How is this reflected in the time and money allotted to the project? If you are not prepared to allow the time, your short-term, unreasonable expectations can sabotage the long-term effort needed.

Ideas Must Find Their Time

Many ideas, including some of yours, are waiting for the time when they will be seen as practical. In the acceptance of ideas, timing is a larger factor than their merit. There is probably a "right" time for almost every idea, but that time is seldom now. Only a few ideas are appropriate for this moment in time; finding them now is what is difficult. Ideas don't age, they ripen. Old ideas become new ideas when the situation changes. *When* an idea was first conceived is less important than whether it can help now. So it didn't work three years ago—what has that got to do with right now? Don't fail to put forth an idea because it has been proposed before. Be guided by present needs.

There are hundreds of ideas tucked away in the minds of the people with whom you work. With encouragement, they will dust them off and show them to you. Many of the ideas are held by people close to the work, maybe even those resisting the change. They are often your best source of new ideas. These co-workers may have been discouraged by the earlier reception given to their ideas, but they still hold those ideas and will give them to you if you have built their trust. Their experience can tell you both what to do and what not to do. You do not always need to follow their guidance, but it is a mistake to neglect them. This may be the right time for the idea that was shelved two years ago.

The Dangers of Rapid Change

People do change, and they change regularly. This is more true of the last 100 years than any time in history. But often we change reluctantly, or only with the conviction we are moving to something better, or because not changing would be too painful. Organizational change is even more complicated because of the many people involved, each dealing with their own issues about change. Given that organizations form around a purpose and delivering predictable outcomes, intentional rapid change runs counter to the way the organizations see themselves working best. Organizations pride themselves on finding the best ways of doing things, and then they do things that way for years. They are not built to move, or ready to move, at an accelerated pace. Often they do not know how. This is a statement of organizational reality. It applies less to brand-new organizations that have a short history, or to groups of people new to each other, or to a small, new organization within a large, old one. But the expectation still applies.

Learn more about the internal rhythms of the organizations you are helping to change. Start with those rhythms, and build on them. Yes, change will be slower than you would like, but if you are building on the established resources of the organization, you need to respect their present pace before you can help them accelerate. Thousands of organizational experiments have attempted to demonstrate otherwise; few have succeeded in the rapid change to which they aspired. Of those that did succeed, it was because they were faced with an imminent, undeniable disaster, and even the high risk of rapid change was the better choice.

Expect a slow pace of change, and it will help you gauge the speed and intensity of the efforts you undertake. This does not apply just to huge projects. It can be a supervisor fixed in her ways, or a board chair who refuses to retire. In any case, adjust the speed of change to the people and organization involved. Be cautious about consultants who claim to be able to change your organization overnight. A highly competitive marketplace has pushed many firms into making claims that exceed their capability to deliver. They think that the way to get your organization's business is to promise fast results. Usually this demonstrates their lack of understanding of organizational realities.

For the moment, assume that your organization, or boss, or coworker, did in fact change as quickly as you wanted. Now, what would prevent someone else from coming along tomorrow with new ideas that result in more changes? This would be the downside of fast organizational change that we often do not stop to imagine. The same inclinations, abilities, or assumptions that allowed your "good" change to happen rapidly would also be available to the next change maker who comes along.

Change in Changing Organizations

Change does not begin and end with you. Your project is just one of many currently moving through this changing organization. One of my biggest frustrations in helping implement change is that the organization will not hold still long enough to apply my fine ideas to it. It keeps changing shape and color and texture and direction, while we are trying to diagnose a problem, come up with a solution, and implement it. We are like parents trying to give a spoonful of medicine to a screaming, struggling, sick four-year-old who won't hold still long enough to drink a full tablespoon. The medicine ends up everywhere but where it ought to be; the child sees the cure as worse than the illness; and the parent ends up using methods that don't seem appropriate to the child's ill health. In the end, the child might have regained health without all the torment.

Let's face it, the organization is not going to hold still. Its movement is not a protest against the "medicine" being administered. The movement comes about because the organization is trying to adapt to what is happening to it, both inside and out. In this respect, the organization is like an organism in its need to respond to the internal and external pressures it feels.

From this perspective, your role as change initiator is not like being a traffic cop who stands out in front and detours the organization in some new direction. You are closer to being a cowhand who throws a saddle on a moving horse as it goes by, cinches it as tight as possible under the circumstances, climbs on, and holds on persistently before attempting to influence the beast. To the extent that we think of the organization as a static structure, we are bound to be surprised. Our models and methods for bringing about change must recognize the state of flux that is the organization. Accepting that it already is changing helps us relax a bit.

Succeed on Their Terms as Well as Your Own

You are not the only one to define organizational success. I know that is not news, but it is important to remind yourself. Your definition of success may be the least important. The real test is whether your effort is succeeding on *their* terms—the terms of the people affected by the change. Think about work you have done of which you are especially proud. Who recognized the success of what you did? What did they say about it? How did that overlap with what you said about it? Is the larger organization respecting your work in ways you want? If you have not established yourself as one who respects and succeeds within the system, people there will deal with you cautiously and see you as an outsider to be defended against. When others know that you want to succeed on their terms, they will confide in you and give you the support you need. This is not to say that you should do everything their way. You need to assert your role appropriately to continue to build your own competence.

We have all seen (or *been*) that bright professional with wonderful ideas that aren't accepted because of the way he goes about trying to change things. Established people in authority find ready reasons to dismiss his good ideas: He doesn't show proper deference, or doesn't follow the rules, or doesn't speak enthusiastically about the organization. The result? Many useful ideas are slowed or stopped on their way to implementation. And the professional with all the bright ideas finds confirmation for his doubts about the way things are done in the organization. He seldom gets the constructive coaching he needs in order to learn that bright ideas are not enough.

Are you that bright professional? How would you describe what success means to this organization on one of your current projects? And how does that fit with your description of success for yourself on that project? How might you satisfy the organization while satisfying yourself? Consider these questions; run your project through them. Chances are, new actions will be suggested, and you will better narrow the gap between the current reality and what you want.

Expect the Change to Allow You to be Yourself

Do not initiate change that requires you to pretend to be someone you are not. As we have said, important change takes a long time, too long a time to maintain a front. Change is so difficult to bring about that you should only undertake it when you are congruent with it. You need the advantage of working in the direction of becoming your better self. In fact, if you do not see the opportunity to learn and grow in this change, you should probably not undertake it. It is the growth opportunity that gives you extra energy and power. Your every action will be congruent with who you are, and that authenticity will show through to others. Successful change leaders do not make it by pretending that the change is important. No. They believe it. They live it.

Think about how this affects your change projects. Consider those that have succeeded or failed in the past. How were those results affected by your clarity about yourself, about what you were getting from this? What evidence do you have that your authenticity helped the change? What do you want to become, and how might this be helped by the changes you are working for?

In summary, these twelve expectations provide a sobering perspective on any changes you might undertake. Probably the largest source of failure in change occurs near the moment of conception. The effort was not well thought out, the people involved weren't invested, they had no idea what they were getting into, the power of the organization was underestimated—all good reasons for failure, and all dealing with the result of not enough reflection early on. Change, organizational or individual, is not easy, and it helps to go in with the right expectations.*

---

*For four more chapters on bringing about change in organizations, see my book, *The Beauty of the Beast: Breathing New Life into Organizations.* Berrett-Koehler, San Francisco. 2000.]

CHAPTER SEVENTEEN

Actions That Get Things Done

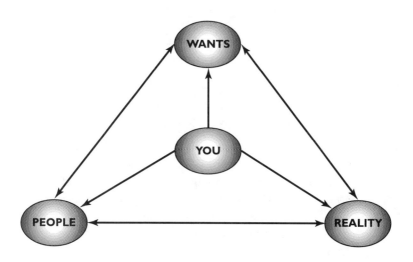

This chapter puts aside the concepts and theories in favor of action. It is filled with examples of ways to get things done from where you are. These pages emphasize the practical aspects of leading people and changing organizations—and they all link back to the GTD model. These twenty actions are for the individual on a work team, group, or committee, that is part of a larger organization. Read these actions with your own work group and organization in mind. My suggested actions will not fit exactly with what you need, but they could stimulate ideas that will work for you. Read the actions slowly; circle those that you might be able to use; check those that you are already doing, and cross out those that you wouldn't consider. Use these twenty actions to help you visualize what you might want to do. Write down actions of your own along the way.

Twenty Actions to Get Things Done

1. Write a five-page paper about what you want your organization to be five years from now. What contribution would you like it to be making? What will it be doing? With whom? What will others be saying about it? What will your group's role be? Whether you share this paper with your work group or the larger organization is your choice. This can be a very worthwhile action to clarify your own thought. Sharing it with your group could help draw them together around a common purpose.

2. Involve your work group in a discussion on the question "What we would like to accomplish around here?" You could use the paper from the action above, or you could pursue this as a separate action.

3. Decide on one action you could take during the next four months that fits with what you really want and is quite different from what you have been doing recently.

4. Talk with someone you work with regularly about your work with them: What do they think of your work? What do they think of the work of your group? What do they want you and your group to be doing? How could you and your group work better with them? Tell them what you really want to be doing and get their reactions. Use this discussion to decide something you will jointly pursue. Then do it.

5. Each month spend time pursuing at least one innovative project or possibility that is connected to the kind of work you are trying to create. Get it on your calendar.

6. Suggest to your work group that together you come up with a project for the coming planning period, something you would all like to do that could benefit the group and the larger organization.

7. Ask people in your work group to assess you as a contributor to the group—especially your interactions within the group: What do you do well? What do they want you to keep doing? What could you do differently or better? What would they like you to stop doing? You can talk with people individually about this, ask the group to talk about it, or you may want someone else to gather this information. However you do it, act on what you learn.

8. If you work for someone, ask that person to look at you as someone who gets things done even without being formally in charge.

Get their guidance as to what you could do, lead, or change that would help you be more effective. In the process, ask what you could do that would help the person you are consulting.

9. Identify one behavior you believe you need to develop and tell your work group that you want their help in doing this. Get ideas from them about what might be most useful for you to do.

10. In the next group meeting, lead a discussion on one of your group's nagging problems. Approach the problem in a way not familiar to the group. For example, if the group usually generates all of its ideas during meetings, do it differently: before the meeting, send each person the key question and ask them to come to the meeting with their answers written down for all to read.

11. Talk with others with whom you work who do the same kind of work you do. Ask them why they work here, why this work is important to them. Seek their deeper answers; get a sense of how their presence here ties in with the larger purposes in their lives. See how their motivation relates to your own.

12. During a meeting with someone with whom you work regularly outside your work group, tell them why you work here, what's in it for you, and how your work fits with your life. Do this well and with feeling. Then ask why they are here, what they get from their work.

13. Suggest your work group meets over dinner to celebrate your work together on a project. During dinner, make a point of telling others how you appreciate what they have been doing. Be specific. Ask them what they have liked about this project. Do not let go of this quickly by falling into joking or socializing.

14. If you regularly lead your group, give a short but intentionally inspirational talk about the importance of your work in your life. Talk about the good points and the bad points. Reveal some of your life purpose in the process.

15. When your work group is discussing a problem, seek a common definition of what it is you are talking about together. Help the group come to agreement on what is really going on before rushing off to solve it.

16. What was the last important project that didn't work for you or your group? Discuss with it with those involved: Why didn't it work? What did it need that it lacked? If you were to do it again, what would you do? Record your learning and set up a way to bring it up before launching your next project.

17. Consider the people you or your group work with: How do you gather information about what they want? How confident are you about the accuracy of those wants? How could you improve on this?

18. If there is another work group or person with whom you feel competitive, meet with them and briefly discuss the effects of the dynamics between you. Then move to discussing shared goals: What do you all want? How could you join in support of each other?

19. Identify at least six key people in your life—inside and outside of work. Spend time with those people regularly. Put them on your calendar for significant blocks of time.

20. Find a chapter of this book that fits with the needs of your work group. Ask them to read it before your next meeting. Discuss together what you learned and what you want to do.

Getting what we want in the future depends on actions like these happening now. All of our grand aspirations and dreams grow from small, practical steps like these, taken daily. By themselves, they don't look glorious or courageous. Together, they form the heart of our work and life.

Building on and Beyond This Book

What can you do to make it a habit—a practice—to reflect on your work and your life? This book has provided you an avenue to do that. I am assuming that, if you want to continue to learn about leadership and change, you will continue to read. The last section of the book offers websites and books that have stimulated my thinking; they might interest you. Always try to be in the middle of at least one book or discussion group that causes you to reflect on your work, in addition to all the other materials you have to read.

What are developmental opportunities beyond reading, in addition to the twenty actions described earlier? Somewhere between actively reading and actively working are many options that help you learn from your experience. Experience is the best teacher *only if* we step back to figure out what we have learned. Many learning options take place outside of work, in a different setting, that helps you understand in a new way what you do at work. Search the Web for sites and discussion groups offered by people from organizations similar to yours, people who face the issues and opportunities you face. Engage with them, offer your ideas, ask your questions. Find people you know outside your organization who have been successful at getting things done when not in charge. Over the next two months, interview at least eight of them. Ask each the same questions, take good notes, write up what you learned, and give a copy to each of them.

Or, consider taking a workshop on consulting, power, leadership, influence, or change. This book offers a consultative approach to change and leadership. If you liked it, then seek out workshops with those words in their description. You can learn more by going off to a three-day workshop that lets you learn and practice. Another option is to lead a learning session yourself. I guarantee that will help you learn! You might want to lead a group of co-workers through a one-hour session on leadership or change. You could use this book and others in the Resources section to design a short session for them. You will learn while preparing the session and even more as you lead it. Design in questions and discussions that help them reflect on their work and understand each other.

These ideas may lead you to other ideas. Notice how many of my ideas suggest that you meet with other people in person, online, or through books, to reflect on what works at work. When you let others know that you are in a learning mode, they become free to teach you and to learn with you. And, you get outside of yourself and begin to see as others see. You *can* listen and learn. Using the approaches I've suggested is usually rewarding for everyone you involve. Everyone learns.

CONCLUSION

A Life Perspective on Leading Change

This book is my dedicated effort to put your work in a life perspective. You want to get things done? Then do what is important in your life. And do much of it while at work. Make your work serve your life. This is your primary source of power, more important than your expertise and the numerous other abilities you bring to work with you. Paradoxically, when you honor what is most important to you in your life, the organizations you work with benefit too. Stay with an organization for a while and the people there will know that when you give your word you can be counted on. They will know that your opinions count because you speak out of your own values, not just trying to look good within the work game. They will know that you choose to be here because this is the best choice in your life right now. And they will also know that external rewards, though meaningful to you, are not everything and not even most important. Being true to your life goals and values will allow you to be a valuable contributor.

As an individual surrounded by organizational turmoil and ambiguity, you cannot waste your time waiting for others who know what's best and tell you what to do. Most of the time, they don't want you to wait; it's your anxiety that is holding you back. Risk more often, always keeping the combined interests of yourself and others in mind. Risk doing what you think is best and you will experience more life at work. We are all still growing up, whether we recognize it or not. Growing takes place within the pressures of daily working and living; there is no escaping that. The challenges and choices you face at work are life challenges; this is your life calling. Through your work you can become your stronger, more courageous self. YOU can reach for what you WANT, while facing REALITY, and working with the PEOPLE important to you. You can aspire to a better organization while accepting its present situation. What comes of doing this? Perhaps some change in your organization. Certainly the transformation of yourself. Live your life and do your work; there is nothing else to do.

Resources

Workshops

Consulting Skills Workshops I and II. Based on Peter Block's book (see below), many graduates refer others to it. Offered by Designed Learning: The Center for Consulting Competence. http://www.designedlearning.com

Positive Power And Influence Workshop. Offered by Appel Associates, appelassoc@aol.com (and others), Atlanta, Georgia. Not strictly for consultants, but for anyone interested in deepening their understanding and skills in dealing with others. 404–255–3200.

Consulting Skills for Professionals Workshop. http://www.consultskills.com Designed by Murray Hiebert (see below) and highly successful with technical professionals.

Books

Bellman, Geoffrey M. *The Beauty of the Beast: Breathing New Life into Organizations.* San Francisco: Berrett-Koehler, 2000. http://www .bkconnection.com If you must work with organizations, are deeply troubled by what they do in the world and aspire to make them better, this book will call forth your idealism and your realism.

Bellman, Geoffrey M. *The Quest for Staff Leadership.* Glenview, IL: Scott-Foresman, 1986. Now out of print, but available used. A forerunner to *Getting Things Done* .... Much appreciated by heads of service and support functions in large organizations.

Bellman, Geoffrey M. *Your Signature Path: Gaining New Perspectives on Life and Work.* San Francisco: Berrett-Koehler, 1996. http://www.bkconnection .com For those times when you or your clients face a career corner that calls for serious reconsideration of life and work.

Block, Peter. *Flawless Consulting: A Guide to Getting Your Expertise Used*, 2nd ed. San Francisco: Jossey-Bass/Pfeiffer, 2000. www.josseybass.com Whether you think of yourself as a consultant or not, Block will help you think through your encounters with people with whom you work closely. Very good on the practical aspects of making agreements with others and building partnerships.

Greenleaf, Robert K. *Servant Leadership*. New York: Paulist Press, 1977. www.greenleaf.org A classic little book that I value most of all for the humble and powerful perspective Greenleaf brings to working with large organizations. A great counter to the "Master leadership" often touted.

Heller, Joseph. *Something Happened*. New York: Ballantine, 1975. I quoted from his novel when writing about risk and fear. Heller worked inside the publishing industry for years. Though dated, much of this material still rings true for large, older organizations.

Henning, Joel. *The Future of Staff Groups*. Berrett-Koehler, San Francisco, 1997. http://www.bkconnection.com Henning has seen it all and is full of challenging, useful ideas.

Hiebert, Murray & Eilis. *Powerful Professionals: Getting Your Expertise Used Inside Your Organization*. Calgary, Canada: Recursion Press, 1999. A how-to book that gives you the guidance you need. Very specific and very helpful to people who are consultants but haven't known it. http://www.consultskills.com

Kouzes, James, and Posner, Barry. *The Leadership Challenge*. San Francisco: Jossey-Bass/Pfeiffer, 1995. www.josseybass.com What I like best about this book is their research. They went out and found what makes a good leader. Guaranteed to stimulate ideas about actions you could take.

Ryan, Kathleen, Oestreich, and Orr. *The Courageous Messenger: How To Successfully Speak Up at Work*. Berrett-Koehler, San Francisco, 1996. www.bkconnection.com Ryan and company have written two books having to do with fear, risk, and courage. Offers very specific ideas, formulas, recipes for action.

Scott, Beverly. *Consulting on the Inside: An Internal Consultant's Guide to Living and Working Inside Organizations*. American Society for Training and Development (ASTD), Washington, DC, 2000. www.astd.org As the title says, lots of stories, advice, wisdom, and tools from an experienced practitioner.

Index

absence, work matrix, 84
acceptance
    expression of, 36
    reality, 104–105
    work matrix, 85–86
accountability, work reviews, 95–96
actions
    courageous, 107–109, 117
    decisions, 36
    gaining respect, 91
    getting things done, 139–142
    GTD (getting things done) model, 6
    initiating roles, 93–94
    political, 51, 53
    taking, 1–2
agreement
    focusing on, 30
    partnership, 71–74
    understanding v., 52
alignment, power, 20
ambiguity, tolerating, 52
anchor, personal life, 101–102
answers, "out there" vs. "in here,"
        103–104
appreciation, expectations, 76–78
arrays, partnerships, 73–74
assessment
    contributions, 140
    partnerships, 73
attraction, work matrix, 85
authority
    limits, 2
    power, 59–60, 84–85
avoidance, problem solving, 31

behavior, changing, 116, 141
boundaries
    expectations, 79
    introducing change, 133
budgets, organizational spending, 56
bumps, organizational, 38–39

celebration, group projects, 141
challenge, daily, 38–39
change
    behavior, 116
    creating, 127
    GTD (getting things done) model, 6, 8
    introducing, 128–138
    life purpose, 20
    motivation, 11–13
    organizational political systems, 49
    partnerships, 81
    people's wants, 26–27
    security, 112
    viewpoint, 78–79
chapters, focus of, 9
charts, white space in, 50
choices
    values, 53
    Work game, 4
clarity
    problem solving, 141
    of vision, 129
    wants, 18, 20
collaboration, problem solving, 30–31
commitment, building, 28–30
competition
    dynamics, 142
    problem solving, 31

confidence, power, 58–59
connections, common, 14–15
consultants, feedback, 97
contracts, partnership, 71–74
contribution, value-added, 74–76
contributors, perfectionists vs., 113
control, the need to, 86–87
courage
    building, 116–117
    GTD (getting things done) model, 118
    to risk, 107–114
    values, 23–24

decision makers
    relationships with, 89–98
    time with, 57
decisions, action, 36
development, personal, 142–143
discovery, self, 101–102
discussions, work groups, 140
disrespect, decision makers, 90
dreams
    focusing on, 13
    reality, 27, 34
dynamics
    partnering, 70–71
    work, 83–87

education, workshops, 143
employees, retention, 61
energy, maintaining, 21
equality, partnerships, 74
evaluaton, validation, 140
exercises
    building respect, 90–92
    courageous consequences, 116–117
    drawing your life, 8–9
    organizational reality, 37
    risk, 114–116
    self discovery, 101–102
    what is important, 14
    work rewards, 124–125
expectations
    appreciation, 76–78
    boundaries, 79
    introducing change, 129–138
    use of ideas, 113
    willingness to risk, 114
experience, learning from, 143

failure
    evaluating, 141–142
    work, 105

fear
    in organizations, 108–109
    personal, 110–114
feedback, decision makers, 96–98
focus, chapters, 9
freaks, control, 86–87
friendship, work relationships, 64

games
    life, 2–4, 102
    organizational political, 48–49
    work, 3–4
goals
    motivation, 11–13
    political support, 50
Golden Rule, partnerships, 81
growth, introducing change, 137–138
GTD (getting things done) model
    elements of, 5–10
    personal perspective, 99–101
guidance, seeking, 140–141

habits, introducing change, 132
Heller, Joseph, *Something Happened*, 108
help, resources, 64–65
history
    organizational, 65, 130–131
    repeating, 29–30

ideas
    timing, 134
    use of your, 113
image, creating a false, 113
implementation, introducing change,
        133–134
information
    gathering, 35
    sharing, 51–52
    withholding, 96
inspiration, purpose, 141
investing, in an organization, 61–63
issues, identifying, 34–35

job loss, fear of, 110–111

knowledge
    self, 105–106
    understanding information, 35

leadership, rewards, 102
life
    anchor, 101–102
    challenges, 145–146

drawing your, 8–9
game of, 2–4, 102
pursuit of purpose, 19–20
taking charge, 21
limits, formal power, 60
listening, difficult relationships, 78–79

maintenance, work relationships, 66
manipulation, tactics, 65
matrix, have to/want to, 84–86
membership, rewards of, 121–122
model, GTD (getting things done), 5–10
money, organizational values, 56
motivation
goals, 11–13
individual, 141

negotiation, problem solving, 30–31
networking, organizational politics, 57
networks, maintaining relationships,
66–67
no, saying, 79

objectives, obtaining, 22–23
opinions, values, 145
opportunities, personal development,
142–143
options, organizational politics, 53
organizations
fear in, 108–109
general dynamics, 136
partnerships, 69–70
politics, 47–49
stability, 127–129
outcomes, organizational politics, 52–53

pace, introducing change, 135
partnering, dynamic, 70–71
partnerships
long-term, 80–81
relationships, 69–70
patterns
rewards, 125
worry, 109–110
people
chapters focusing on, 9–10
employee retention, 61
GTD (getting things done) model, 6–9,
100
resources, 62–63
perception
negative, 91–92
power, 58–59

perfectionists, vs. contributors, 113
perseverance, implementing change,
133–134
perspective
common, 41–43
life, 145
personal fears, 110–114
picture, 10 year, 19
planning, priorities, 55–60
plans
creating a 5-year, 139–140
organizational financial, 56
politics
organizational, 47–49
personal, 49–51
position, source of authority, 85
power
alignment, 20
attribution of, 2
authority, 84–85
building formal, 58–60
dynamics of, 58
Life game, 4
resistance to change, 131–133
praise, accepting, 123–124
precedents, introducing change, 130
presentation, introducing change, 131
priorities
decision makers, 96
planning, 55–60
problems
group solutions, 141
restating, 42–43
solution acceptance, 30
projects, initiating, 140
purpose
partnerships, 70
pursuit of, 19–20

questions
coping with answers, 26–27
focused on potential partner, 78
GTD (getting things done) model, 7–8
what is important, 14
who makes a difference, 61–63
"Why is that important?," 11–13

reality
accepting, 104–105
chapters focusing on, 9–10
discovering, 33–37
dreams, 27
GTD (getting things done) model, 6–9,
100

reality *(continued)*
  organizational, 37, 53
  political, 48
  reaching a common understanding,
    42–45
  shared sense of, 37–38
recognition
  achving, 76
  alternatives to, 122–123
reflection, on work, 142–143
relationships
  difficult, 78–79
  long-term, 80–81
  open, 65
  partnerships, 69–70
  personal differences, 74
  political, 51, 57
  web, 65–67
  working, 28, 63–64
reluctance, work matrix, 84–85
reputation, building a successful, 75–76
resistance, to change, 128, 131–133
resources
  authority, 60
  help, 64–65
  people, 62–63
respect
  decision makers, 90
  earning, 91
  expression of, 36
  introducing change, 137
  organizational history, 65
responsibility
  control, 87
  personal, 102–103
  risk, 115–116
reviews, work, 95–96
rewards
  leadership, 102
  types of, 119–123
rhythms, organizational, 134–135
risk, courage to, 107–116
roles
  formal power, 59–60
  initiating, 93–94
  partnerships, 70
rules, organizational poltics, 51–52

satisfaction, intangible rewards, 123–124
secrets, organizational politics, 51–52
security, change, 112
self-awareness, increasing, 105–106
solutions

acceptance, 30
  organizational reality, 37
Something Happened (Heller), fear in organizations, 108
speed, introducing change, 135
stability, organizations, 127–129
statements
  focus, 104
  "I" vs. "They," 102–103
  written mission, 27
success
  anticipating, 71
  organizational change, 136–137
  partnerships, 73
  rewards, 120
  visibility, 75
support, formal power, 59–60
systems
  linking work into key, 94–95
  organizational political, 49

tactics
  changing, 140
  manipulation, 65
  problem solving, 30–31
time
  change implementation, 133–134
  with key people in our lives, 142
  organizational values, 56–57
truth
  discovering the, 36–37
  reality, 104–105
  redescribing problems, 42–43

understanding
  reaching a common, 42–45
  v. agreement, 52

validation, evaluaton, 140
values
  building respect, 91
  choices, 53
  follow the money, 56
  mission statements, 27
  mixing with poltics, 50–51
  opinions, 145
  work, 23–24
viewpoints
  changing, 78–79
  decision makers, 92–93
  political, 51
villages, organizational, 43–44
visibility, success, 75

vision
    10 year picture, 19
    clarity, 129
    mission statements, 27
    personal, 102

wants
    chapters focusing on, 9–10
    common, 27–28
    discussing your, 17–19
    diversity, 25–27
    fulfillment time frames, 22
    GTD (getting things done) model, 5,
        7–9, 100
    identifying group, 142
    motivation for change, 12–13
web, relationship, 65–67
wheel, reinventing the, 29–30
why
    is *that* important to you, 14
    motivation, 11–13

work
    control, 87
    dynamics, 83–87
    failure, 105
    game of, 3–4
    human element, 61–63
    intangible rewards, 122–123
    internal v. external rewards, 119–120
    partnerships, 69–70
    reflection, 142–143
    relationships, 63–64
    reviews, 95–96
    values, 23–24
workshops, learning opportunities, 143
worry, patterns of, 109–110
wrong, fear of being, 113

yes, saying, 79
you
    chapters focusing on, 9–10
    GTD (getting things done) model, 6–9,
        100–101

About the Author

Geoffrey M. Bellman has never been in charge. From his first fourteen years inside major corporations to his last twenty years as a consultant to the for-profit and not-for-profit world, all of Geoff's work has been in service to others' goals while simultaneously working for his own. He has worked as a systems analyst, a human resources generalist, a business researcher, a trainer, and a director of a corporate function. He has consulted to hundreds of organizations—companies, agencies, and foundations. Much of his earlier work focused on renewing large, mature organizations. Over recent years, he has reduced his corporate work and now gives much of his consulting time to community organizations.

Besides *Getting Things Done When You Are Not In Charge,* Geoff has written four other books:

The Beauty of the Beast: Breathing New Life into Organizations. (Berrett-Koehler, 2000), focuses on what we love to hate (and hate to love) about organizations. . . All the mystery and madness that surrounds succeeding with these creatures.

Your Signature Path: Gaining New Perspectives on Work and Life. (Berrett-Koehler, 1996), a book for reflective individuals working through significant life change.

The Consultant's Calling: Bringing Who You Are to What You Do. (Jossey-Bass, 1990 and 2001), a book for those who want to know what consulting is really like as a career, a living, and a life.

The Quest for Staff Leadership (Scott-Foresman, 1986), a book for staff, service, and support people in large organizations everywhere—and winner of the National Book Award of the Society for Human Resource Management.

Geoff is a co-founder of the Community Consulting Project, a group of Seattle-area consultants and learners who offer their expertise to not-for-profit organizations. He belongs to the Organization Development Network, the American Society for Training and Development, and the Woodlands Group.

Geoff grew up in Washington State and left in the sixties after completing his graduate work at the University of Oregon. He and his wife, Sheila Kelly, followed work around the country to Denver, New Orleans, Tulsa, and Chicago. In 1981, they moved their family and the consulting business to the Pacific Northwest. Their three children have grown and left home. Geoff and Sheila live in sight of Puget Sound and the Olympic Mountains and are unlikely ever to move again.

Contact Geoff at 206–365–3212 or at gbellman@aol.com.

Also by Geoffrey M. Bellman

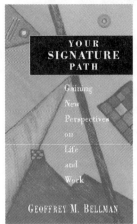

Hardcover, 178 pages
ISBN 1-57675-004-3
Item #50043-375
$24.95

An excerpt from
Your Signature Path

This book is about the mark you are leaving on the world, the difference you make. It does not to assume grand or small ambitions for you; it does assume that you want to use your time here thoughtfully. You want to be proud of how you live your life and the want to grow in the process of living it. You care about becoming yourself more fully and wish to contribute to the world as you do it. And that love and work are important to this.

I have spent my life in the pursuit of good love and good work. This book is my best statement to date about combining these. The book will mention both frequently; it will link them, marry them, as I believe they ought to be married. My primary focus will be on work because that is the realm I am comfortable writing about and where my years in the work world qualify me. Work and love are both essential to life and essential to each other. They are too often unnaturally separated in the work place; this is my small attempt to rejoin them. I have a strong belief in work's potential as a path to our individual greatness—and I know that may not fit with your experience. I suspect it fits with your aspirations and that is why this book could attract you.

This book strengthens your ability to see your path. It is more about seeing, and acting on that new sight, than it is about gaining brand new skills. I hope to help you use your present skills better by affecting how you see the world. I am confident that when you see what is going on around you differently, you will act accordingly. I will help you see by asking you to look through different lenses from those you ordinarily use. Sometimes those lenses will be mine; others you will cut and polish for yourself.

In short, it is for busy, invested people who care about the difference they are making. It may be a book for you; it is definitely a book for me!

Also by Geoffrey M. Bellman

THE
BEAUTY
OF THE
BEAST

Breathing
New Life into
Organizations

GEOFFREY M. BELLMAN
author of the bestselling
Getting Things Done When You Are Not in Charge

Hardcover, 250 pages
ISBN 1-57675-093-0
Item #50930-375 $27.95

An excerpt from *The Beauty of the Beast*

Organizations are the world's twenty-first century dilemma. They are magnificent and mad, wonderful and wretched, crazy and compelling. They make so little, and so much, sense. Never before has humankind been able to bring together so many global resources within common form and purpose. Our ability to create organizations exceeds our ability to control them; they have power beyond imagining.

Organizations are a personal dilemma as well. We rely on them and rail against them. They promise us gratification; we promise to pay within ninety days. They lend us their resources in return for our loyalty. We search for our meaning through them as their suppliers, customers, workers, citizens, beneficiaries, and victims. We live in hope and fear of their consequences. We are living that science fiction line, "We have created a monster!" Whether named agency, or government, or health care, or education, or corporation, we all live and work around these beasts. All of them, but especially corporations because of their accelerating power in the transformation of the global marketplace.

The book's title alludes to the fairy tale in which a merchant gives his pure-hearted daughter to the Beast in exchange for his own life. Belle, the daughter, despite her initial horror, chooses to look for the best in the Beast and gradually finds it. In fact, she finds fulfillment where she at first felt revulsion. This book is for the Belle in each of us, encouraging us to face and find life where we stand, to choose in this moment to create the next. By choosing, we breathe the new life into organizations that we all so urgently need.

Who this book is for...

Many of us are as intrigued with the potential of organizations as we are disturbed with the reality; we are drawn into relationship with these bureaucratic beasts out of necessity and attraction. Millions of us join our personal purpose with organizational purpose, hoping for the best and making the most of this uneasy marriage... for better or for worse, for rich or for poor, in sickness and in health. We live in the struggle for our meaning within structures that were not built with us in mind.

Many of us recognize how essential organizations are to what we have achieved and what we will become; we see the immense potential they represent. We know they figure in the future of life on this planet. We are part of a highly educated work force that each day steps into organizations that have not caught up with what we have learned about ourselves. We seek our actualization in organizations put together for other purposes; we feel our schizophrenia as our minds and hearts proclaim the possibilities and our organizations proclaim the limitations. We are seeing more attempts at creating productive organizations filled with human accomplishment and spirit, but there is so far to go. This book is for people who know this line of thinking and want to continue it.

The book helps you step back from organizations to ask: Why do we keep creating these creatures that fall so far short of our dreams for them? What is our role in doing this? And the book helps you move in close to consider why you give so much of your life to these often frustrating and occasionally exhilarating beasts. This book helps you imagine what people can do together and how they might do it. It engages you in thinking about what you could do at work, and offers you ideas on how to do it. It guides you in a personal and organizational exploration in search of purpose, contribution, community and identity. Its many questions open you to answers you have not yet considered while its content will inspire your daily work. This book helps you embrace the organizational world as it is while working hard to change it.

Berrett-Koehler Publishers
PO Box 565, Williston, VT 05495-9900
Call toll-free! **800-929-2929** 7 am-12 midnight

Or fax your order to 802-864-7627
For fastest service order online: **www.bkconnection.com**

Also by Geoffrey M. Bellman

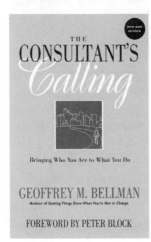

Paperback, 238 pages
ISBN 0-7879-5847-6
$20.00

The Consultant's Calling
New and Revised Edition

How do you thrive as a consultant, contribute to the world, make friends, and become the person you want to be?

Through this book, I ask this question of every element of your work. My own consulting career has been a search for the answers to this question. I am bringing the question to you, as well as my best answers to it. The question is not, "How do you get clients and make money?" As important as those two goals might be, they mean little if not in service to contribution, friendship and integrity. When this book considers getting clients, it do be with my question in mind. When the book looks at making money, it will be with my question in mind. Your approach to organizations, clients, and change will likely be altered when you see them through my question.

You can use a career in consulting to enhance your life balance, personal growth and happiness—if you choose. That is what I have been doing for over twenty years as an independent external consultant. This book builds from my experience, suggesting what you might do to shape a life for yourself with consulting near its center. You are creating a life for yourself right now; this book will help you think about that life, what you want to create and how to go about doing that.

The Consultant's Calling is about responding to the voice within, the voice that calls us to pursue meaning and purpose in our lives. This book recognizes the possibility, even the necessity, of achieving much of that meaning through our work. Given that we spend many waking hours working, it makes sense to put those hours in service to a motive higher than money. Given that changes, struggles, and growth are part of the human work experience, why not benefit from that experience in personal as well as profitable ways? Why not recognize our consulting work as a path that leads toward meaning in our lives?

The Consultant's Calling is available at your favorite bookstore or from Jossey-Bass Publishers at **www.josseybass.com**